Broken Promises

One Woman's Pain is Another Woman's Experience

Freda Camille

Copyright © 2023 Freda Camille

No part of this book may be reproduced by any means without the written permission of the authors.

All Rights Reserved.

ISBN: 978-0-9912415-9-0

<u>Broken Promises</u>
<u>One Woman's Pain is Another Woman's Experience</u>

Freda Camille

Table of Contents

Foreword
Introduction

Monique
    A Reflection in Solitude — 2
    Into the Light — 5
    Broken Promises — 6
    Thoughts — 6
    Reality — 7
    Perfect Accusations — 8
    Pieces of Me Broken — 9
    Insomnia Thoughts — 10
    Broken Promise — 11
    An Afterword for My Broken Promise — 12

Tiffany
    The Heist and the Heartbreak — 18

Michelle
    Broken, But Not Beyond Repair — 42

Chantel
    Perfection is an Illusion — 54

Loveberry
    The Value of a Promise — 62

Kiara
    Broken But a Promise is a Promise — 73

Tureka
    Broken Promises – True to Self — 82

Lauren
    Relationship Addict — 90

Dara
    Trust in God's Promise   96
Janie
    Forever Tanya   112
Anna
    Joy Inside my Tears   128
Tekeisha
    Toxic Friendships   132
    Friends   138
Tracy
    My Truth   142
Katrina
    A Promise Broken   150
Sheila
    Full Circle   164

Meet the Authors

Foreword:

An American poet Muriel Pukeyser asked: "What would happen if one woman told her truth about her life?"

My response to this question? Undoubtedly, the world would split open!

Broken Promises greatest accomplishment is the honest and deep understanding of the acknowledgement and release of the faithful imitation of who we are in order to awaken our true selves. The insightful narratives of challenges and untapped strength-once unveiled- joined forces with healing energy. Through these narratives, gifts bestowed upon us by our Creator were revealed and reclaimed!

Each narrative I read, I paused to breathe in and breathe out; "I knew these women" I thought, I traveled their journeys. I smiled, eager to get to the next shared experience of shortcomings, waiting to read about the moment of discernment; the epiphany which showed up just in time to assist her to overthrow the paralysis of her spirit; now free, to realize her authentic self.

This piece of work is absolutely absorbing and gives legitimacy to the power of women and the perseverance of the human spirit. It is when our intentions are determined to release the faithful imitation of ourselves, we are able to build up a new woman and a new generation.

"The world would split open" means we would take ourselves and our experiences seriously and grow from them and dance when all were watching! The women and their narratives of *Broken Promises* have split open their world and are about to change your world.

Stay on the journey. I hope this book will help to create your inner peace and freedom.

Emlyn DeGannes
Mejah Books, Inc
2083 Philadelphia Pike
Claymont, DE 19703
302.793.3424

Introduction

Promises are made to be kept; it helps build trust and integrity. However, we know sometimes that doesn't always happen. Just think about how many times someone has promised you something, or the promises you've made to yourself and to others. Are you still waiting for the commitment to be made complete?

Broken Promises is a Collaborative Book detailing the cause and effects of how disappointment from unfulfilled expectations of "Promises" can have a negative effect on you. Each author gracefully pens a story of triumph and faith encouraging her readers and each other through a new awareness and acceptance of self-reflection and self-love. Often we find that "one woman's pain is another woman's experience "; and through transparency we are able to help others find their own path towards healing. The circumstances we face reveal opportunities for us to overcome and now freely share our stories with the next woman who is beautifully broken and suffering in silence with her own issues.

It's time to break the cycle and… be free!

Monique

A Reflection in Solitude

Don't quite understand how I still feel so alone
Words just sit on my tongue and
      taunt me like the school yard bully
Thoughts run rampant in my head
Scattering everywhere and nowhere at all
Chaos
Presented in a pretty little package
Wrapped up in a bow of a smile
I'm an outsider within the reach that
      I have created for myself
Straddling between ignorance and awareness
In a constant struggle with faith and fear
All the while knowing that the battle is not only
senseless, but not of my responsibility to pursue.
Idealistic thoughts constantly chase me
Realism laughs a hearty scoff in my face
My heart is full of emptiness
For fear of being laden inadvertently
      with the indication of wrong
Lips rest in an awkward position-
Between effective movement and ineffective use-
tantalizing scandals desires with careless wisps of
ignorance escaping-as we all at times are guilty of
The mirror is cracked.
It no longer offers a reflection,
      so I must bear the task of remembering.
Thinking back to a time that
      was never really thought of.
Just acted upon.
Lived.
Trying to capture glimpses of effortless care,

when the heart, mind, and soul
were virginal-unscathed.
Unaffected by this thing called life and
the mess we often create
when we try to participate without guidance.
A time when nonsense was not only unnecessary
but also unacceptable.
When there truly was not a care
because you just-were.
There were no titles and no expectations.
If you made a mistake
you learned from it and moved on.
Even laughed along the way.
A time when tears were lessons and scars healed.
Circumstance was experience.
And experience was the Teacher
at the front of the class called life.
And. Life. Just. Was.
Movements were slow.
Not really mattering
if they were calculated or purposeful.

And as she lives, she tries to piece together
her mirror so she can see her reflection.
And for one moment, see herself.
Not just look, but truly SEE herself.
Absent of all the titles and expectations put upon her-
regardless if by others or self-imposed.
And for that brief moment; if she finds it, she can breathe. Stand up tall.
Enjoy the momentous empty peace of mind.

And see herself.
And once that is done.
Once she captures even the slightest glimpse...
Then she can continue living life for herself.
And celebrate the titles.
And create expectations- for herself.

I need to press pause
      so I can gather the pieces to catch a glimpse.
Because I feel it slipping away...

Into the Light

No matter how much the darkness tries to cover
Light always wins
Navigation of a new space is scary but so
necessary
Showing someone,
you deserve more than the all they thought you did
Is taking your life and
creating newness in a space that's unfamiliar
It's having the audacity to say no more
To stop pretending that someday the smile will come
back
To stop suffering and yearning for a simple touch
A consequence of love
To act on this is to justify that you are enough…
Even if you're the only one who understands it
Step into the light
Darkness bears no fruit.

Broken Promises

The biggest promise we break to ourselves is not being who we set out to be. It's like going into a store and picking a version of yourself off the shelf that matches the situational expectations or requirements of others. We are not expected to be whole unless we are broken. Then we are promised that all the pieces will magically come back together. Not for us, but for our benefit and benevolence to others.

You promise yourself that you'll be more intentional, softer, wiser. However, as soon as a version of you is needed, you step up because trauma bonds with trauma.

Thoughts...

You never know how scarred you are until you remove the bandage. In this case, the bandage was masked in comfort. You know, the comfortable "consistency" that you pretend is real shit to make it palatable and realistic....

When you rip a bandage, you leave behind skin. It's a rule. In bad relationships you leave behind pieces of you.
It's a rite of passage,
Teasing you until you get it right.

Reality

No matter how much people tell you otherwise, if you don't believe it, their words fall idly at your feet.

No matter the accolades received, recognition or encouragement, you STILL never think you are enough.

Always a missing piece.
Always a need to improve.
Not in the manner of reflection, but as a mode of survival.

Debilitating.

Trying to locate some imaginary picture of self-imposed expectations draws breath from your existence.

Takes the glow from your cheeks.

You cannot tell if your mask is visible. Detected.

You walk the tightrope of having it all together. With sharks of mediocrity swimming below.

Smiles turn into exasperating breaths
    behind closed doors.

You lie to yourself a million times a day.
Constantly trying to catch a glimpse
    in the mirror of what others see.

Blind.
Struggling to be sufficient.

Searching for the validation of your own adequacy.
Wishing you could just be.
Enough.

Perfect Accusations

You accuse me of being perfect as if striving for excellence is a disease which I caught from someone else and brought it home to you

Pronunciation of the word rolling off your lips with such venom

My pursuit of perfection is a fallacy to you
Because all you see is imperfections
Because that's
All
You
Have
To
Offer
Your blemishes, sorry's, and your mistakes
Content with the bullshit
Excuse me if my pursuit offends you
Go spit that useless shit somewhere else...
You're in my lane. ✌

Pieces of Me-Broken

Shattered pieces of a past she once knew
Trying to fix and put them back together
Hands bloodied
Picking up pieces and both sides are jagged
A thousand motives of trust broken
Heart
Broken
Trying to figure out what's going on
Where the picture was ripped
How the mirror of life dropped
Shattered
A
Million
Pieces
Picking up the pieces to start a new
Fighting thru the pain
Hands
Bloodied
Scarred.

Insomnia Thoughts

And just like that...
    she realizes why she feels the pebbles under her feet
Why the devil is winning
Why tomorrow is tomorrow's tomorrow come again
Why this journey has become haphazard with
    twists and turns
Like the fight had left
Just like that
She sits back to reflect for a moment
All that has gone awry in life
She realized
She's gone AWOL from Gods army

Hung up her fatigues
Fearful of the glimpse of greatness shined upon her
The finish line
Turned a deaf ear
Traded prayer for just doing it
She realizes she was doing nothing at all.
She realizes
She was
Doing
Nothing
God
Was...
Searching for her uniform
Asking Him for forgiveness
Stepping down from herself
To give
Herself

Because without Him

She is nothing
Proof
Facts
Real ish...
She realized.

Broken Promise

Sometimes you just have to get out of your own way. There are just things which you cannot control, you must learn how to take a breath and learn to release it-even if for the moment.

Ego is crippling. At time we can be our own binding. It comes disguised as a thing we think we can control and morphs into a rude fallacy which can leave us breathless and paralyzed. Shocked.

Today I choose me. I am sure I will need to remind myself of my choice, and I am sure that today will not be the last day I have to state loudly this choice- for my own belief. I chose to stay home. I felt broken and of no use to anyone in this capacity. That is what I am known for and what I must stand in daily- my usefulness to others.

This is not life as I planned. As I sit here and think, I do not even think that my life ever had a chance to be planned. Like many other women, life is planned for us based on choices, circumstances, and opportunities. This is not the life I will lay down and accept, for I understand that I am God's choice. To have faith in Him is to understand his exponential plan for my life...a life that allows me to feel full.

I hid in relationships and service. My worth is determined by my value to others. That is a dangerous path to carve. Once there is no service to render, self-worth may be a topic that is up for review and deep reflection-or not.

I am wonderfully made.

I am purposefully made.

To be anything less is to break a promise to myself, from God.

Who am I to be anything less than a promise?

An Afterword to My Broken Promises

The worst promise one can break is one you make to yourself. When we are young, people ask you what you want to be when you grow up, you know- the proverbial future plan conversation which seeps from the lips of every adult to your brain from about the age of five. Though the question is not sent with the intention of malice, it unintentionally begins to teach us those expectations of others exist and will eventually become a part of our decision- making process as we age. How awesome would it be, if, from an early age, we are asked "what makes your heart happy?" How many lives would change if granted the permission to delve into our own lives for the sole purpose of seeking purpose and discovering what makes us move?

I have broken loads of promises to myself in the search of pleasing others- or worse, the assumption that actions and decisions made on my part would have such an impact on those around me. This is the furthest thing from the truth- and it took me 44 years to even scratch the surface of learning.

The promise that I broke? Not believing in ME. I stopped being my own champion and touted my accolades on the effect that my actions of service had on others. I was not only a mother (at 19, graduated, and homeowner by 21), I mothered hundreds of children through my career in education and in the community. I prided myself in how I saw myself through the eyes of my family and my students. I wore a mask.

Do you know how hard it is being what you think everyone else thinks you are good at being?! Yes, read that again...I did it because everyone thought I should. Do not get it misconstrued, I LOVE what I do. However, my acts of service may have looked a bit different if I had been brave enough to take more risks. Working in education is risky, but the classroom became a safety net for me. I did not do any work of innovation; I simply was the teacher I needed. Oh, I know I was amazing, but if I pushed myself, I could have been Marva Collins amazing. I could have had that school I wanted to establish in order to help our babies flourish in this thing we call life.

I often dusted off that mask just to get through another day of doing what I thought I was good at. The first risk I took was leaving the classroom to go into administration- again, because we are trained that that is the next part of the journey.

Enter March 13th, 2019...Covid. This thing literally stopped the world, and for a moment, I had the freedom to breathe and think. When you are left idle for two weeks, there is only so much time movies and ordering online can take up. Left to sit with my thoughts, I realized that I could not continue to exist in a cycle of broken promises. It was time to break the mask. I sought therapy (GASP...yes, black girls seek help too!) and began the journey of promising to be my most authentic self.

You are now reading my second biggest risk. Those who truly know me, know that I have been writing since I was in middle school. I remember my Godfather laughing at the cover of my journal when I was 13, because I titled it "Chronicles of Mo". He asked me how I could have lived long enough to have a 'chronicle'. If he only knew what my teenage heart and mind was suffering through- the earliest stages of the creation of my mask. Writing for me has always been a salve. It may sound cliché, but if you know, you know. I loved to read, and still am a voracious reader, but writing just allows me to explore and release thoughts from deep in the recesses of my mind. The page has always been my safest space. Though I know many, there have only been a handful of people who have been permitted inside my safe space of verbal reprieve. When encouraged to share on a grander scale, I always shied away, reflecting on the feeling I had when sharing my work with my safe adults- they are just words, and you look like you need help. Yes. That was the sentiment I was left with, so the safe space became a smaller world I thought not worthy of sharing.

Enter a special friend who did not take no for an answer, and a therapist who allowed me to capitalize on my healing hobby...and now you have these pieces. This journey was the final promise I made to myself and refused to break. You see, if I had to do it all over again, I would be a published author and motivational speaker. That is what I have wanted to do (and still can!) These pieces have been written over a decade, but show the journey that I am taking to get back to Mo.

The pieces represent cyclical parts of my journey: times when I had to straddle the fence between what I believed and what I needed to get done; times when I was walking a tight rope trying to get through the process of hope, realization, and actualization, times when life was a seesaw and the person on the opposite end was in control; times when life was a whirlwind, and I allowed myself to be whisked away by hope in action.

Even in this process, I almost allowed another promise to be broken. Procrastination took over and I suddenly had writers' block. For the entire duration of the project, I wrote everything except on the assigned topic. It was a challenge to release pieces of me that most had not a clue into my world. It was a challenge to be vulnerable. To be open. To be on the receiving end of feedback and thoughts of others. It was a challenge to face my fears. On the due date for submissions, I was literally dragging my mouse across the screen, mind invaded by negative thoughts. I almost talked myself out of it. I had nothing worthy to share and was willing to allow this opportunity to pass me by. I set out to call Freda to say thank you for the opportunity, but God took over and I simply was honest. As my statements of disappointment and self-sabotage evaporated from my lips, my heart opened. I wept. I cried for the little girl who was too afraid to share the very thing that often saved her life. I cried because I did not think I had enough thoughts to fill up a page. I cried because I did not see myself worthy to be published. I cried. She just listened. I was granted the affirmation that my feelings were valid and experienced by many. I was affirmed. I was consoled. I was provided with hope and belief, and I was cheered on to just keep going. This was a part of the process that was so necessary. This was the part of the process where my fears were washed away with those final tears and feelings of not being enough. This was part of the process I didn't know I needed.

This is a final word to my broken promises:
You do not define me. Broken things can be mended.
I am healing.
I am here.
-Mo

Tiffany

The Heist and The Heartbreak

Have you ever heard of a bad incident that involves someone you know, and it shakes you up? How about a robbery of a home? A person being involved in a home invasion, or their personal things taken from them? A heist is just unlawful right? How about if it was your life that was hijacked and taken on a wild ride? I didn't realize, but early on in life I had been attacked, not physically, but emotionally for sure. God knows your end from the beginning, and so does the enemy. It was a long time before I realized that my life had gone off the rails from the plan God had set for me. I was way off course due to me mentally not seeing myself in the right manner, the self-love tank was empty, and I was allowing people in my life that would eventually hurt me. I have had to deal with a lot of scars, unseen by the eyes, but each one left pain to conceal. I had learned to wear a mask for my heartbreak and pain, I had become an actress acting as if I was okay.

As I encountered this new awakening of what I was missing I also had come to a painful reality of why I wasn't properly loving myself. I had settled into fear, doubt, and shame. My past actions were mostly based on fear or trying to make life happen all on my own. The fear and lack of love for myself had my mind robbed of my God vision, and I was lost. I am not sure why I thought I could function outside of God's plan and course that he already had set up for me. Why wouldn't I trust in the one who created me? I now understand that there is no sustaining victory without God!

I found myself many times on the bedroom floor crying out to God once again after yet another failed attempt at this thing called life. I would be brought to my knees by my own choices and circumstances. Yet again I would heal up just enough to go out again only to make another bad decision. My awakening changed my life a few years ago. I realized that my life wasn't my own, I was failing horribly at it, and I couldn't keep doing things the way I was. I would never get to the big wins and blessings in life without letting God lead me and guide me through. He tells us that his Word is a light to our path, so he holds the plans. A light switch finally came on in my heart and mind! I realized that my life and legacy was dependent upon me making different choices. It was time to heal internally and take back what had been stolen. I decided to finally have a healthy fear, and it was a fear out of reverence for God. I now know that the scariest place to be is without Him!

As a pre-teen, a series of events happened. I believe that these years and the events that took place would alter my life-and not in a positive way. Being a mother, I know the importance of foundation. I don't proclaim to be a perfect mother because there's no such thing. Now, I am able to see the cracks in the foundation of my own life which allowed the heist to take place. The late 1980's into early 1990's was really formative due to the things I was exposed to. My parent's divorced, and I had way too much freedom as a young girl. (Now don't get me wrong, there were some really great times. Those were the years of watching rap videos, so you could replicate the dances at the next party. The days when you wore door-knocker earrings with your name in the middle. The times of wearing the latest and greatest trends in fashion from clothes to sneakers. I believe the 1990's set the bar for fashion in relation to hip-hop, and I enjoyed every bit of it.) This time period for me was major in other ways. My parents were searching for new lives individually, and as the oldest child I was given the responsibility of taking care of my siblings after school. Starting in the sixth grade, I became the babysitter due to my mother's evening shift. My father, in addition to being newly single, traveled a great deal for work. My siblings and I got picked up every evening and dropped off at my mother's apartment. Free time for me lasted from after school until I had to be picked up at our grandmother's house. Let me tell you, I was everywhere I wasn't supposed to be! I had always been a great student. But what got me was no one ever asked where I was from the time I left school until the time I arrived at Grandma's house. My job was to be at my grandmother's house in time to get those kids home for homework, dinner, and baths. I understand my parents needed my help, but this situation cultivated a negative effect. I felt unattended as a teen, and it seemed like my parents were too busy for me even when they weren't working.

I began to look for attention elsewhere. With my newly gained freedom, I began to enter a world my parents knew nothing about due to my freedom, and

I began to think differently. I had grown-up responsibilities, so therefore, I began to think I was old enough to do what adults do. I started hanging around people and places where drug activity was occurring. I began to associate the fact that there was this glamorous life attached to what I saw; from the fly cars to the flashy clothes and jewelry. Also, I spent some time on the weekends babysitting for a few of the hustler's girlfriends when I didn't have to watch my own siblings. I found myself intrigued with the stories I would hear and the cash I would be around in their homes. So, as my parents were figuring things out in their own lives as divorcees their oldest daughter was falling into a world they couldn't have imagined. During my tenth-grade year of high school I began to date a young man. Once my parents found out they despised the relationship, and definitely tried to end it. The issue was they really couldn't. They were too busy with work and other things. I ended up pregnant. The most hurtful thing is as I was caring for their children, I was forced to get rid of my child. That tore the veil between me and my parents. I had already grown accustomed to hiding everything from them, but once I was forced to have an abortion, that attitude transformed into full-fledged defiance. "How could they break me?" I would ask myself. A few months later I was pregnant again, and this time I told my parents I would not be forced to get rid of my child. I became a mother to a son at the age of seventeen, my junior year of high school. I fell in love with the game. Fell in love with a guy involved in the game and had what I thought was everything in my young mind. I had no clue about life, or how things can change so quickly. I had the popular guy, the fly clothes, jewelry, and our son. But what was to come is exactly what my parents told me would happen... heartbreak! So, now I was broken hearted by the guy I loved as well as my parents, and I just wanted to run away. I felt betrayed by everyone! My son remained a place of love for me, and his life gave me a reason to not give up. He continues to be such a joy in my life. (He is something I would never change about that time period!) Truth is, I didn't know it then, but the minute I gave my body away in those young years I was betraying myself along with my future. I added more cracks to my foundation in those years by my choices. I was off God's plan for me, and I felt it. I had been raised to know God, and I attended service every Sunday as a child throughout my teen years. I accepted Christ in my teenage years, I would know I was on the wrong path, but I would keep on going. But I fought through my pain and set my eyes on something new. I found out that I could leave my little town by way of furthering my education. I continued to keep my grades up, worked hard to take care of my son, and my next goal was college!

I got accepted to a few universities, but I chose Delaware State University since it kept me close to home. My grandmother and her sister, Myrtle, kept my son during the week so I could attend college. I would come to Jersey on weekends or pick him so he could stay with me on campus. I went and asked for permission for my son to stay on the weekends with me on campus, just so I could stay away from my hometown. My Grandmother told me to go get my education because no one could ever take it away from me, and she was telling the truth! DSU became my new place to be free. I formed what would be lifelong friendships, had new experiences, and it gave me the ability to dream again. I was able to put the hurt behind me and move forward. My first semester went well, and I went back to DSU after Christmas break as planned. I got a call from my Aunt Peg that would change my life shortly after settling into school for my second semester. She called and told me she was picking me up, my mother was in the hospital, and that it was serious. My mother had been diagnosed with leukemia that March, and she passed away a few months later in July of 1996. My mother, Anita, was only thirty-six years old. My new title was guardian of four siblings. The enemy had robbed me again. My mother was gone, another crack in my foundation. As my second year at DSU was about to begin, my head was spinning. I now was a homeowner, a mother to my son and now my siblings; and trying to figure it all out without a clear path. I didn't even know how to balance a checkbook! I also had another problem, and it was my father. He was still traveling and wanted me to focus on the care of the children. He refused to pay my college tuition. My mother made that a stipulation while she was alive, but Mom was gone, and I had to figure this all out. I decided to withdraw from DSU and figure out another alternative for my education. The day I arrived on campus I ran into a guy I had previously met through some friends. He asked why I was on campus so early, I explained the situation, and he told me I could pay for school myself. He took me to the financial aid office, and I was able to get my own loans for college. The guy that I had only occasionally been around that helped me that day would end up becoming my husband, and the father of my two amazing daughters.

Delonao and I would figure life out for us once we became a couple. He not only helped raise my son, but he also helped with my siblings. He came into my life and jumped right in the mix. Please know I didn't always make it easy for him. Hurt had taken up residency in my heart, and I couldn't see that he was trying to love me. I eventually got it together and let that man in to love me. We had a few love and war episodes along the way, but thank God, we made it through. We had our first daughter as he finished his master's degree, and I finished nursing school. I eventually came home and finished school at the Community College. It was a lot driving back and forth from New Jersey to DSU for classes. Also, the responsibilities were heavy on me, and I needed to be close to home. Together we set our goals in motion. The plans came together as only God can do. He eventually came to NJ to live from NY, and began his career working in Delaware. We were building our home, and planned our wedding. I graduated just as we got married. It was all coming together, and life was exciting! The wedding was such a great time! Our families still talk about it! We had three hundred guests, a great honeymoon, and one month later we were in our new home.

Our marriage was never perfect. It took a lot of hard

work and some therapy sessions, but you have to know who's worth fighting for in this life. Delonao was worth fighting for as well as the future of our children. I so wanted them to have what I didn't have. I wanted them to see and feel a sense of security and love by two parents in the same home.

Delonao had always been a motorcycle rider from the day I met him, and he continued to be a cyclist throughout our relationship. One morning he kissed me on my cheek and left for a ride with his sport bike club. I would never see him alive again after that morning. He had been in a terrible accident that he wouldn't recover from. That summer day would change our lives forever, and we had just found out the week prior that I was pregnant. So, here I am twenty-four years old, no mother, no husband, another child on the way, and once again trying to figure out my life. The Word of God tells us that the enemy comes to steal, and he was robbing me.

I look back on my life and he was trying to destroy any faith I had been taught. My faith wasn't what it is today, but even in those times I still knew God wouldn't do that to me. I had acquired another crack in my foundation with the loss of my husband, and this time it would affect my children. A woman that loses her husband not only loses a partner, but a whole lot more. A husband and father stands guard over his family, protecting them, guiding them, emotionally supporting them, and financially supporting them. Our lives had been flipped upside down, and this momma had no idea how to figure it out. I did know that I couldn't just succumb to another one of the enemy's plans to defeat me.

As a widow life looked different on every level. I realized there were many things I didn't know how to do from landscaping to budgeting. My husband was the breadwinner and the money manager for our family. I was the one that executed the plan for our family as the wife and was the spender. Delonao always had to reel me in on the spending and the budget. I set my children's college funds up, secured more life insurance on myself, and after that I had no plan. I know now that you have to plan to survive this life, or life will continue to wear you down! My second daughter was born, and my plate of responsibilities continued to grow. In addition to the children and my siblings, I also cared for my grandmother along with her sister. I had all this to do while having a huge void, hurting, and heartbroken. I began to make a lot of mistakes. These mistakes would cost me way more than I realized. These decisions would lead me even further away from God's plan for my life.

My goal was to mask the pain, act normal, look the part, keep it all together, and I became a great actress. I made sure that me, all the kids including my siblings looked great, they were in activities of their interests, and I continued to work hard. I wanted my children to still have what me and Delonao imagined for them, but I was now on my own to navigate life. I wasn't always the best parent. Later on when my children were older, I actually apologized to them for various things. I used to yell at them instead of talking at times, and I never thought how this would emotionally affect my kids. I was an emotional train wreck on the inside, and I realized that it was important to acknowledge my children's hurt. We cannot heal what we refuse to acknowledge, and I wanted my children to be better than me. I wanted my grandchildren to have emotionally stable parents, and not carrying hurt from their grandmother. It's amazing how far an apology will take a relationship. I would continue to shower the children over the years with things, trips, and fun activities. The truth is nothing could fill the void of not having Delonao in our lives.

On top of all that I had a couple relationships that were really emotionally unhealthy. From the very beginning I would state my expectations and that I wanted marriage again. I wasn't living God's way, so how could I expect his results? I wanted God's vision for the family without having the required components. I wasn't receiving love appropriately, and if I'm honest with myself I couldn't call it love. I was accepting whatever they were dishing out all so I could hold on to something that was hurting me with the possibility of a "Mrs" title. I was so desperate to get the title of, "Mrs," again I let myself stay in these relationships way longer than I should have. I am talking years! In my mind I believed that being a married woman was a necessity for respect. My love for myself was non-existent, my self-esteem was low, and I was allowing myself to be mistreated. I was still trying to look the part focusing on my outer appearance all while my spirit and soul were suffering. My life was essentially at its lowest part by the end of 2015. I had to sell the home I had built for my children, file bankruptcy, and financially I was in the worst place I had ever been. I was still trying to cover it all up even to the children, but I knew in my heart I was in a really bad place.

On Thanksgiving Day of 2015, I had an awakening that only God could do! I realized that I was attracted to brokenness and believed that because I had not been so perfect in my life, I didn't deserve proper love. My whole life had been a series of robberies, and I was listening to every lie of the enemy. Me not believing that I was worthy of love was the ultimate heist. I was empty, tired, heartbroken once again, and the sad part is I had broken my own heart by accepting less than I deserved. I knew many times not to make the choices I did, but I was too busy focusing on what the world was doing instead of God's way. One thing that happens when you accept Christ as your personal Lord and Savior, He never leaves you, but I had left Him to follow my own way. I was in service every Sunday, active in the ministry serving on our healthcare team, but not following God's system outside of those couple hours on Sunday. The relationship was over by the New Year of 2016, and I was moving forward trusting God with my life. My focus was God, my children, finally completing my bachelor's degree at DSU, and working hard to keep our heads above water financially. What happens when you decide to totally give your life to Christ, but things still manage to fall apart? Well, it happened to me, and guess what? I still trusted God!

I had a new outlook on life, I was still not financially secure as I wanted to be, but we had what we needed. I mentally was in a great place and happy!

I decided to not date for a while, be celibate until marriage if and when that happened, and I did eventually remarry years later down the road. But I had no idea that my marriage would be doomed-literally from the very beginning. A month after we were married there would be a set of events that took place out of our control, and we would end up not in a good place. How could two God-fearing people not have a successful marriage? Well, people is the key word. There are principles you follow as married couples to get through hard times, and we didn't carry them out successfully. There are absolutely no perfect people, I have forgiven, and moved on with my life. I will say that when the separation occurred, I was devastated because I didn't see us ending, but divorce would be the finale. It was in the midst of the pandemic, and here I was in another low spot. I was emotionally dragged, and this time my faith was in its greatest battle! The reality was that my marriage was over, I once again had nothing financially, and I had to rebuild my life from the ground up. I once again was wearing a mask because no one knew what was happening in my life. People would tell me all the time how they admired me for all that I had been through in life and how strong I was. The reality was I was emotionally frail. I thought that I had finally found my love, but here it was just a cruel trick! I had done it the right way, God's way, and the marriage still failed. I was alone, and the enemy was whispering every negative thought he could to me. He was bringing up all my inner most ugliest thoughts about myself that no one knew. I was under attack, and so was my faith. I had been heavily studying the Word, was given the privilege of teaching the Word of God, testifying about God's goodness, and the enemy thought that my failed marriage would put my spiritual fire out. It almost worked.

Worry is an unrealistic fear. The ride it takes you on is definitely a scary one. I had let it enter my heart. I would gain nothing by worrying, but I did anyway. I spent a year after the separation anxiety ridden and in despair as if I had no hope. I was crying nonstop as soon as I was alone. In an attempt to avoid facing the reality of my new life, I stayed busy, taking on more hours at work. On top of all the loss my body was physically ill. I had major hair loss, stomach issues, and depression was looming over me waiting for me to give up. But God! He never let me go! He would show up through a friend, a song, a sermon, or a scripture verse that would uplift my spirit. I began to fight one day at a time just trying to get to the next, and my strength was becoming renewed. I realized I wasn't alone in this life. God still had a path for me to travel, and it was a new one just for me! I had gained a lot of weight, so I began to exercise again consistently, sought therapy, and went to specialists to get my health back on track. Stress and anxiety will wear you out physically and mentally, but I realized I needed to fight! I could not show my children I was a quitter, and I needed to let them know that we win if we stay in the process! I not only needed to recover for me, but I needed my children to still trust God. I knew that my life's recovery would have God's hand all over it. I needed them to see the goodness of God! God will do a thing, but he also needed me to take the steps physically in my own life. I praised and worshipped. I prayed, I sang, I shouted, I screamed, and I screamed out for his help! God showed up every time! He had my back, and in those times of worship I would feel the presence of the Holy Spirit. I knew that a lot of my trauma I had experienced throughout my life was inflicted on me by others, but it was still my responsibility to seek healing.

There are things that will show up in your life including people that will break your heart, but it will fix your vision. You need to be able to see right spiritually, so that you can believe right, and love right including yourself! This new sight will lead to the necessary steps of the removal of people, places, and things that do not serve you. I asked God for help to see right, hear right, and speak right. I asked for his help on removing those that shouldn't be in my life, and he did just that. There are some people that shouldn't have been in your life in the first place! They were never a part of your story, and those people need to remain a part of your past. My losses woke me up, it was vital for me to make good choices, and to set boundaries in my life. I was also on a new path of self-discovery. I was out to learn and master myself. I needed to believe and trust in myself. I realized I had been setting myself on fire for others while my own light was fizzling out. I needed to rejuvenate myself and speak positive affirmations to myself. I didn't even believe what I was speaking over myself at first, but then one day I did! The new parameters I put in place allowed me to not only survive but thrive! I needed to be a woman of perseverance and hope. I was loving myself finally! I was no longer looking for love and acceptance in others. I realized that God's love and acceptance was all I needed. God loved me freely, and I didn't have to do anything to get it! I just needed to fully accept and believe it in my heart. The love was there the whole time!

The next step was figuring out where I was going, and what would be the next steps of my recovery for my life. I didn't have all the answers, but it was my faith in God that I knew would get me there…wherever that was. I believed that God would direct my path, I am confident in his Word, and all his promises. I took his Word personally. I read the bible as if He was speaking directly to me. I believed then and now that God is taking me somewhere, and I could not go back to the people that had emptied me out! The people that robbed you, used you, lied to you, aren't in Hs original plan, so don't go back there to pick them up! Yes, we are here to forgive. We are to give grace…absolutely! I can promise you that nowhere in God's Word does he tell us to be a fool. There needs to be new rules followed going to where God is taking us, and it's all for our protection. We have to analyze our life, sift through what remains, and see who makes the cut to stay. We need to look closely at our own behaviors. I believe if we sit with ourselves long enough, we learn a lot, but many times we don't take the time to just be quiet. It's necessary in our reset and recovery period to self- evaluate, take personal notes on yourself, and see what improvements need to be done.

I realized that I was sick and tired. I forced myself to take accountability for myself! I asked myself, "what did I have on it!" How was I gonna put skin in the game to prove to God I was serious about my own recovery and next level? Accountability is major, and people will place blame on others instead of looking at ourselves. Once you invest in yourself, God will move, and He wants to see you engaging with Him. Are you reading The Word, are you praying, and are you taking the time to praise? I realized I could silence the enemy by doing all those things, especially praise and worship time. My spirit and soul could not stay in a sad place during that time of praise. I would then watch a sermon or two in a day's period, just so my ears could hear a positive message. God's Word is set up to guide, protect, and help us to make better decisions to win in life. I wanted victory on every level! When you are out of compliance with God's system how can you get God's results? His Word and ways of living gives us the assistance needed to get to our success. I can tell you that outside of God is a lot of pain, increased failure, and lots of disappointment. I'm a proven fact and proof that doing life outside of God's will is nothing but despair.

So, we have to stop saying what was done to us, and

ask ourselves, "what am I going to do for myself?" The world's system may be fun at the moment, but it's a trap. The sabotaging comes from our own hands at times. We have to control what we can and set our own trends with God at the forefront of it. Also, don't be so set on achieving goals that you sacrifice your integrity to get there. There's a price to pay when we do that, and these choices can be detrimental to your future. God at times is growing us up in that time period of waiting. He's building us up and preparing us for when opportunity arises. We have to stop the cycle of doing things within our own power, falling down, and then going back to God for help. If we only would stay in God's process, we would have less heartache and regret. We have to slow down, have patience, and know that God's path for us is lit up with nothing but goodness. So, weigh everything before you step into a thing because it really may cost you more than you want to pay. Hell may break loose all around you as you follow God allowing him to be the director of your life story. Know that there's nothing, he won't protect you from as you follow him. He wants to complete the work that He's begun in us. He needs to have full control of our lives, and we need to have full confidence in him to complete the performance. He has planned it all out for us from the beginning of our existence. He has saved us from every fire lit furnace for such a time as this! I realize now that through it all He was keeping me alive, covering me, and protecting me even when I wasn't living right for this moment right here! God has a plan for me. It involves talking about his goodness and love. It saved me!

In my life's reset and recovery I have learned to focus, communicate effectively, listen on purpose, pursue my goals, and recover my life with God as the head of my life. I am fully invested with him! I am not halfway in and halfway out. I am not lukewarm! I am on fire for all that he says I am and has called me to be!
I am unafraid...FINALLY! My God!

I spent so much time afraid of just letting go, and I am not sure why. Surely God made the heavens and the earth, so He clearly doesn't need my help fixing my life. God is so patient with us even when we grieve Him with our actions. He patiently waits for us to allow Him into our lives, so we can hurt no more. God is pure love. I realized that I was wonderfully made and full of every good thing he's determined for me to be. I am His ambassador here in the earth, His representative, and I will tell my testimony of freedom for others to become free. I overcame it all by His love, mercy, and grace! How can I not trust Him and be fully confident after I know all this? My new reality is love, joy, peace, and VICTORY!

So, be confident in God, and what He's doing in your life. Don't let life's occurrences show up and dictate to you who you are! Don't allow life to reduce you! We are so much more than our past, or even our current circumstances! God says so! I refused to allow my pain to turn myself pitiful. I knew I was stronger than that. The enemy will try to bombard you with distractions, old history replaying in your mind, burdens, bills, or anything he knows he can use to throw you off. The enemy tries to wear us down and wear us out! The enemy knows all the old ways we had, and the people we were attracted to that pulled us away from God. We have to strengthen what remains and press forward in our faith. We continually fight from a place of victory, we just can't quit in the process, because we know that the fight is fixed! God is undefeated! He not only fights for us, but He protects us, provides for us, and comforts us! Reading God's love letter to us, the Holy Bible, will keep us focused on our goals. God tells us in His Word to cast our cares on Him. He tells us how He's no respecter of persons, and He will confirm His work and plan in us. It's a part of our survival kit! You have to fill your heart and mind with the tools necessary to defeat the enemy when he comes for you. In order to have peace you need to carry God's Word and principles in your heart. We can't get through this life living in this world without them, and God's Word helps us to maintain our peace. God intended us to have Eden, but that is not our current reality. Most of the manuals we are given in life whether it's for our car or computer we never read them but let God's Word be an exception to the rule. It was my complacency in life that stalled my future. I spent more time focused on everything and everyone else but God. Our success is in the changes we make, the stretching of ourselves, and taking ourselves out of mediocracy to discomfort. The discomfort of change is necessary! God wants our commitment and conduct to be in alignment with him. He really is trying to see how much we are willing to be focused and committed to get to our purpose in and through Him.

In my awakening I knew I had to make the necessary changes and adjustments in my life, and I continue to make them as needed. I'm more aware of myself now more than ever before. I confront myself when I see something is out of order, and it's important to allow people that love you to speak into your life. You can't get through this life alone...no one can. You need a safety circle. These people love you, but aren't afraid to confront you if they see you doing something wrong. Honestly, whenever I was out of pocket by saying something or doing something wrong, I already knew it. One thing about having a relationship with God: it won't take long before He drops in your spirit to correct you. I will automatically feel bad when I speak or do something out of line. The truth may be uncomfortable and may sting a little emotionally when you are getting corrected, but it's for our betterment. It's time to recognize, react properly, and stay in restoration mode. I want it all back! I want everything that the enemy has stolen from me, and I refuse to take my eyes off of it. I had lost a lot financially, spiritually, and personally. I made a decision to recover it all, extract the truth, concentrate on my purpose, and commit to my covenant with God. I now have a plan! I have worn many titles in my life from widow to teen mother, divorcee, and certainly more but I refused to let life devour me. I now let God have it all. My past, my present, and my future all belong to him. I know I am home now, and in a place of safety. Who's bigger than God? No one! I'm finally in a relationship with the one who has mattered the most from the very beginning of it all!

Life now has promise attached to it. I wake up now every day with expectancy, live as light, and give out love freely. I'm pursuing the life God has for me. He has filled me up, and my goal is to pour it all out so that people will know how great He is! I now find myself in quiet seasons where I feel and know I need to sit still, listen more, speak less, and focus on the next thing. I didn't understand it at first and was looking for people to be around whether it was family or friends. I finally got the picture! My quiet seasons are for me to concentrate on myself, I knew my family and friends were a call away, but I needed to focus on "Tiffany!" I now actually enjoy my alone time and do so on purpose. I know now that loving myself and being intentional towards myself is important to thrive. I also realized that it was okay to not belong to anyone. I didn't have to be dating, or in a relationship. I was focusing on the cultivation of a new me, and I needed time to do that. I no longer focus on my life disappointments, heartaches of the past, or the broken promises to myself. I made new promises to myself. I am basking in the fact that I no longer desire what doesn't love or serve me. I am continuing to learn myself, continuing to evolve into a better woman, and loving those in my life that have proven they loved me. I am committed to myself! I owe me! I am happy and full of joy. I realize now, and it's so sweet to say, "I am enough!" I am worthy of every good and great thing that God has stored up for me! I also refuse to allow my past to affect how I act and show up for myself in the future. Healing has been vital, and I am on a total wellness mission. My objective now is to forgive quickly, give grace, and live such a transformed life that people will have to say God did that! I'm expecting God to do a wonder in and through me! I have freely given Him my heart to do His surgery on. I can't recover it all without giving it all to Him! I welcome people in my life now based on an assessment, because not everyone needs to go where God is taking me. I love everyone, and there are no perfect people. But I am well aware now that people get allowed into my life based on their integrity and personal performance. The quality and protection of my present and future is at stake. I will not compromise! I have realized my worth and it is non-negotiable! It's imperative that regardless of the relationship that I receive the God kind of love that I am entitled to wrapped in respect. So many times, in my life I sacrificed my joy to exchange it for pain. God has opened my eyes to see properly, and once you see properly you will never want to walk through life blind again. The heist and the heartbreak is over, and the King of Kings reigns forever more in my life!

-Tiffany

Michelle

Broken, but not beyond repair!

There is a little girl in every woman and often she is overlooked. So, my story begins with the little girl in me. I was conceived and birthed out of a broken promise. My mother was young and while staying with a friend, she was violated. This violation produced an unwanted, unexpected blessing, which felt more like a curse. I was conceived in pain, so there was a pain that I was born out of. Because of the incident, my mother was rejected and had to experience the journey alone. Her life as she knew it, ended. A broken woman, carrying a "burden" wanted to abort the violation. However, when she requested the abortion, she was denied. I can't imagine how she truly felt, but I felt what she went through because I was in her womb.

At a young age I remember leaving my elementary school to walk to Family Court. As I am entering on the right with my mom, this man who I did not know, but gave us eye contact was coming out on the left side. He did not speak, but his presence felt familiar. Inside the courtroom I had to give my blood because we were there to do a DNA test because I was not being accepted. The image hasn't left my mind since that day, and the feeling of wanting to be accepted follows me every day of my life.

Fast forward from the little girl to the young lady. The little girl who did not get the approval of her father became bitter! I was beautiful on the outside, but hurt and angry on the inside. I received a call from my father after I returned from a mission trip, and I was so excited to hear that my father wanted to see me. So I reached out and planned to come and see him for what seemed to be the first time since the little girl crossed his path on the steps of Family Court. However, when I arrived at his residence my father never came outside to see me. Instead, he opened his bedroom window and dropped some money out of the window down to me. I remember talking to my best friend at the time who went with me because I couldn't understand how someone who talked about me and wanted to see me wouldn't even take the time to come outside his house to greet me. I used the money that he dropped out of the window to go buy me a new pair of Liz Claiborne shoes. They were cute, black with a bow tie on the top. I remember wearing those shoes like it was the best thing that I had ever gotten in my life because my dad gave me money to buy them. Just like the relationship that did not manifest over the years, the heel of my shoe that broke off while I was walking down the street reminded me of our broken relationship. I was angry because those shoes were expensive! They represented acceptance in my mind, yet their fragile foundation quickly showed me how my relationship with my father, who rejected me, and didn't really show me love, was broken.

The broken little girl who grew into a bitter young lady became a bruised woman. The rejection of my father impacted my childhood and made me cautious, reserved, and distanced. The fact that I was raised without my dad, I did not trust men! If my own father did not want me, then why would someone else want me? Dating was not my strong point because not only had I experienced rejection, but I grew up seeing physical abuse in the form of domestic violence. I vowed in my heart to never attract a weak man because if he attempted to put his hands on me, he would not live to tell it. The little girl in me never healed, which prevented the young lady from fully blossoming.

I remember as a young adult attempting to date. I had a gentleman asked me why I was so bitter. When I heard him ask that question, I immediately resorted back to the little girl in me because I couldn't really answer why I was bitter I just knew I was strong. I always protected myself by preventing anyone from having the opportunity to hurt me. After trying to start a relationship with him, that eventually faded. I became more involved in the church serving, leading, and maximizing my time. Shortly I started becoming more and more hopeful that some great man in the church would recognize my potential and maybe then I'd be loved and accepted. I served in every capacity that I could. I remember a time when I went to church Sunday morning with one outfit on and then Sunday evening I came with another outfit on because I wanted someone to find me, to love me, and to become the missing piece of my heart that never received validation.

One night a minister of God was preaching and he called an altar call for healing. I stood in that line and remember him saying that God was going to send someone to heal the place of my father. I remember weeping and crying because no matter how much someone tells you to get over it, they would not understand the power of rejection from birth, unless they've been through it. You may be asking where the broken promise in this story is, but the broken promise began at my conception. At the moment my mother was violated at a young age; the moment I was denied of my bloodline, the more I grew and the more bitter I became. They tell you fathers are supposed to love their children; fathers are supposed to be there to protect them and to show them who they really are - yet I didn't have that and I felt like it was because of something that I did, when in reality, it was something that he was responsible for.

After years of desiring to be loved and not really receiving the love that I wanted, I began to imagine if one day I would become someone's better half. I had some potential relationships that ended okay. I say okay because to be honest they really didn't go any further than friendship. Then one day the bitter little girl who became a bruised woman was approached by "the man of my dreams." I clearly remember the night that our eyes crossed, and my heart leaped - it was during the time I was grieving, and I couldn't shake the feeling of still wanting to be loved.

I remember the moment when he said, "if you just say the word – I'll leave everyone else alone." To say I was flattered at the time was an understatement! In all my thirty plus years – no man had made me a priority. Yet here was a tall, handsome, gainfully employed man pursuing me. Now I can't begin to tell you what he saw in me because I was not interested in his pursuit. I really did not plan to give him the time of day. Eventually, later that year, I invited him over to my house for pizza and a movie. That was the start of what seemed to be a promising future. Imagine finally thinking that you have been found. Found by someone who is really interested in you for the first time in your life. Don't get me wrong, there were some gentlemen who would act interested, but they wanted one thing or the other.

That evening when he showed up, we watched a Denzel movie and ate pizza. I remember we sat on opposite ends of the room. He was on the couch, and I sat on the love seat. We simply enjoyed each other's company. Imagine me being in my late thirties and inviting a grown man over my house, but not being able to interact like an average adult woman. We talked for a little bit and then I packed up some snacks because I was going to be with family for the holidays. He assisted me with loading up my car and he thanked me for a decent evening. For the first time in all my years of desiring to be loved, I received a Merry Christmas text, which lit up my whole day because I was on somebody else's mind.

His pursuit was just the beginning as he started slowly finding the way to my heart. It was a breath of fresh air because he wasn't like anybody that I had met before, yet he offered me a sense of stability and hope for a beautiful future. We had so much in common but were different in many ways. What started out as a friendship continued for close to ten years. A lot happened in those ten years, but most of them were enjoyable. When we made it official, I realized that the little girl in me, needed to be healed in order to be made whole. There were times that I was difficult to love because I feared rejection and disappointment. And although I did not tell him my entire story, he made me feel like he was the man who would help the little girl become a better woman.

When I met him, he told me he was a man of his word. For the most part he honored that commitment, and I did not have an issue trusting him. But one day I sensed a shift in our relationship, and I couldn't really grasp what happened or when it started happening. Have you ever had that feeling in your gut that you knew something wasn't right, yet you shrug it off and trust that it will work itself out? Well, that's the feeling I got one day and although I never had a prior relationship, women's intuition let me know my hope no longer existed.

It was the month of my birthday. I hadn't seen him for a while, and he invited me to dinner. Because I felt something different, I didn't enjoy dinner that night. He sat beside me, and I felt he wanted to tell me something, but he was unable to form the words. At the end of dinner, we walked to our separate cars and said goodnight. I began to ache on the inside. This wasn't the guy that approached me, and I couldn't figure out what changed, but I knew something had changed. There were a series of events which happened after the meet up that really tried to crush me. Within a matter of a week or so, the inevitable truth showed itself. My knight in shining armor had cheated with another woman and he did not have the courage to tell me. If I could tell you how it was all revealed, you would probably give me a gold medal.

The moment I discovered what he did, I was crushed. I lost myself to the point that I had my friends incited and I couldn't really tell anybody else the story because it was painful. There was really nothing he could say or do to heal the little girl in me. The fear of rejection resurfaced all over again – all because he made me a promise there would be nobody else and yet he cheated. She revealed it; and he could not even give me a reason why. I think that's the least he could have done for me since she was the one who showed up to tell me about their relationship.

You are talking about a sister being broken all over again – yes that was me! I was grieving the loss of my parents; I was struggling to get my life back from all the painful moments that transpired prior to this – and I did not even get a chance to understand what drove him to cheat on me. No one could prepare me for what I experienced because I did not deserve it. The little girl in me has cried enough and now she was traumatized all over again. My feelings of failure, rejection, disappointment, and abandonment began to creep their ugly heads in my space.

It has been a few years and I am forever grateful to know that the Potter wants to put me back together again! I've been broken, bruised, and bitter – but I am now bigger, better, and blessed. I have always been blessed, but I have not always felt blessed. There is a difference, especially when you are going through life and experiencing turbulence. I know that I am not the first young lady to be rejected and abandoned by her father or cheated on by their significant other, but one broken promise if it is not addressed, will lead to a life of brokenness.

Today I write this chapter, which has so much more to it, but for the sake of sharing my broken promises story, I shared what I believe would help someone else out. Although I shared the story of my father's rejection and a mate's deception, I can share that God allowed my father and I to connect before his death and that little girl, was healed. I can also share that God allowed me to forgive the man that broke my heart, and we remain as friends. Broken promises should never become the bottomless pit in your life. Make them a beautiful platform to empower, encourage and ignite others in their journey of spiritual, physical, and emotional healing.

Broken Promise Affirmation:
Hello Beautiful, pick your head up. Forgive the offender and remain good to yourself! Don't let someone else's struggle become your story! Remove yourself from bad relationships; Remind yourself of your potential and reclaim your time.

B is for Becoming – You are always becoming the best you; you will be!

R is for Recovering – You are recovering from the pain someone put on you!

O is for Overcoming – You are daily overcoming the trauma you have experienced!

K is for Knowing – You know the truth and it will set you free!

E is for Enduring – You have endured enough, now move on!

N is for Newness – You can start something new whenever you need to!

P is for Purpose – Your life has purpose!

R is for Reflecting – You must reflect on the positive rather than the negative!

O is for Organizing – You must organize your life for your success!

M is for Motivating – You must remain motivated to live your best life now!

I is for Insisting – You must insist on making you a priority!

S is for Standing – You must take a stand to keep your sanity!

E is for Emphasizing – You must emphasize to

everyone around you – that you are the priority!

S is for Soul-Searching – You must do a soul search whenever you feel you are losing you!

Signed,

-Michelle

Chantel

Perfection is an Illusion

At the age of 10 I remember my Uncle William telling me I had a million-dollar smile. Since that day I took that as a challenge to mean I would be a millionaire one day. It wasn't what he said that made me sure that this would happen, it was what he didn't say. What he didn't have to say is that even at such a young age there was a light inside of me that he saw and when I smiled it allowed the world to see it existed. I can remember so many moments in my life that people in my life expressed these high expectations of me and who I would become one day. It's amazing to come from a foundation of loving people that built character and confidence. My parents instilled confidence, values, and morals from a very young age. I was expected to exceed the standard, never fall subject to bullshit and reach heights others might only imagine. I was their version of a prodigy. No, I wasn't naturally skilled in athletics or musically inclined, but at some point, someone decided that I was gifted. The problem with being held to a high esteem is you are beyond making a mistake. No, it doesn't mean people don't expect you to be flawed in any way, but when you are they give you a pass- over and over and over. Every mistake you make takes just a little bit more from your existence. You internalize your faults, and you begin to tell yourself it was all a lie. You start to realize that the perfection you always thought was attainable…truly does not exist in the real world, and the real world doesn't give two shits about little old gifted you. I say all this to help paint the picture of how things can start out so amazing and quickly spiral into "what the fuck" in a split second. But they promised me I would be great!

College is supposed to be a time of finding yourself, exploring new opportunities, and making lifelong relationships. My experience at college unlocked all my insecurities which led to a breaking point. I chose the nursing field as my major because I remember being told when you are a smart woman you should be a doctor, lawyer or nurse. Now, I realize there are endless industries in which intelligent women are needed and leading. Nursing seemed like a place where I could care for others while feeling fulfilled. I couldn't believe how difficult the coursework was for me. I tried to get help, but the professors were not very supportive. I am grateful that a mentoring group for black students provided me with a student mentor and a professor in the science department or I would have never made it through any program at school. I finally realized that I chose the wrong damn school. I remember hearing people talk about how predominantly white schools needed to meet a quota of minorities to maintain funding, but I never wanted to believe that to be true. Once I became a junior in the program and new mother it was evident that they did not think I belonged there. Honestly, my grades were not the best, but I was getting by the best I could. When my son was born, I planned to continue to program and graduate on time. The program refused to let me stay on course, forcing me to take a semester off because they thought I needed some time to acclimate becoming a mother. I didn't need time, I needed to keep moving forward so I could complete the nursing program and move onto to the next phase of my life as a single mother and college graduate. I had never received the support I needed while in the program, but it helped that I had a few friends in the cohort to tutor, support and love on me through the struggle which was just enough to help me get by. Now they had taken away my lifeline and I had my first experience of discrimination as a young black single mother. They thought that they could break me!

The plan that I set for myself had changed drastically. I found myself living back home while raising a newborn and trying my best to finish college. This was not the perfect picture that I had imagined, this picture was flawed and unfinished. I found myself in a dark place months after taking the required break from school but caring for my son gave me hope and strength to keep going. I applied to an Historically Black College or University, known as an HBCU, to continue the nursing program. When I was accepted everything seemed to be right back on course. It was a week before the semester at the new school would start when I received a call about my new schedule. I happened to be on my way to the school that day to complete some paperwork and financial aid. The woman informed me that although they had accepted all but 8 of my credits, I would be a second-year freshman in the actual nursing program. She proceeded to tell me how the credits would be reflected on my transcripts. (As if that mattered when you just told me I would lose over two years of education basically being forced to start over.) I was pissed! Not only did I waste my time and excitement on this school that was supposed to be for me, but now I had to return to the damn school that did not have a place for me to begin with. Ultimately, I did what I had to do. I returned to the first school and took alternative classes- while now off track and behind for graduation. I continued to work while in college and by the time my son turned one, I was able to secure my own housing. I had purchased the first car in my name with my grandfather's help. It was a brand-new black Ford focus hatchback. Before moving to the new home, I gave the car to my grandfather and decided to get something without payments. Well, his daughter decided she wanted the car, but little did we know the payments never got made and the car that was in our names got repossessed. It was like finally, things seemed to be moving in the right direction and here comes the devil. I had no idea how long he would linger this time or hell maybe he never left. This was all too much for me, so I decided I needed a break.

When my friends started talking about a trip to Florida, I was reluctant at first because the timing didn't seem right and too many of us planned to travel together. It had been a long time since we all had the time and money to do something fun together. We went to Miami, and it was like all of Delaware decided to follow that week. We had a great time until the night we split up and decided to do our own thing. I had met some ball players earlier in the week, so they took me and one of the other girls to a club. After the club, we went back to the hotel with the guys and finished the night there. We were extremely drunk and last I remembered one of the ladies had fallen asleep in a corner. It was one of the wildest nights I ever had, but it felt freeing to do something I had never done before. We met up with everyone from the group late night and I sat with a friend from Delaware on the beach and watched the sunrise.

We all had our secrets from that trip, but we agreed that whatever happened in Miami stayed in Miami. As the trip was coming to an end, I received a call from home. My friend that I let stay at my house got into an argument with her child's father after he found out she had company in the house. He tried to attack her while she was in my car. He busted out all the windows and damaged the exterior of the vehicle. Now remember I lost the Focus, but I had replaced it with a split color Lexus ES 300 with 22- inch rims and a system. My fun weekend had come to a complete halt and reality of all the drama at home immediately set back in. I returned home and had to deal with a busted-up car. Little did I know that the drama was only beginning. Days later I received a call from one of my homeboys asking me about what happened in Miami. He was concerned stating that someone told him I was videotaped while in Florida and the tape had made it back to Delaware. I was confused because I did not know what he was talking about or how he could know details about what happened in Miami unless a recording actually existed. The details of that weekend were supposed be a memory, left in Miami. I could not believe that footage existed of what

I had considered to be a trip where I could be free from my cares and expectations. Knowing this information made it almost twelve hundred miles back home had me in a chokehold. What I left there was never meant for anyone to discover. This was my breaking point...

I was numb. Everything that I had dealt with started to flood my mind all at once. I felt like I was drowning. As I looked at myself in the mirror, I did not know the person that was looking back at me. All hope for positive outcomes for me started to fade immediately and I felt stupid, alone, and empty. I grabbed a bottle of pills off the dresser and took the entire bottle. For a moment, it felt like I would finally have some peace, but that moment faded when I realized I had a little one playing in the other room. How was I going to leave him? He did not deserve to have me leave him in the world I brought him into. I called the police and told them what I had done. They rushed me to the hospital, gave me cups of charcoal and admitted me. This was my first experience with therapy. I was the youngest person in the therapy groups, but I felt comfortable talking about my troubles and leading the discussions. Many of the other group members were executives. They had been working at the largest bank in the state and recently lost their jobs to downsizing. We found ourselves all in the same desperate place trying to find a way to cope with how our lives were going. My therapist and I were able to work through many layers in the time we worked together. She eventually, told me that I was on the wrong path. She believed that my calling was being missed, she suggested that I become a therapist. And at that moment my future seemed promising again.

-Chantel

Loveberry

The Value of a Promise

The question was once asked, "What does Broken Promises" mean or look like to you? And that's where my mind began to spin. Spin to the left then to the right then I had to rewind and rethink from the beginning of times. Broken Promises can mean and look different in everyone's eyes but once you're done reading this book ask yourself what does broken promises mean or look like to you.

As a child we were promised things by our parents, loved ones, teachers, friends and siblings. As a child when things are promised we hold tight to them because a promise means it will, must and going to take place. While we are promised things, we place our trust in the hands of human beings. When those promises are fulfilled, we are delighted and filled with happiness and continue to put our trust into those individuals.

So in our minds as a child, we place those individuals in a special place because they fulfilled what they promised. No matter how big or small they keep their promise!

But when someone doesn't hold up their promise, that is where the BROKENNESS begins. When individuals make a promise, they sometimes don't even think about the ability to actually fulfill their promise. They hope that they can and sad to say some even just say it in hopes that you might even forget about it. Either way once a promise is made, we believe.

When the promise isn't fulfilled but is excused with another promise the heart tends to give the individual another chance. After so many chances you lose trust in the individual. Then our little minds at a young age becomes altered without realizing now there is a trust issue all because a promise was broken. When promises are broken, we may become angry, heartbroken, isolated and sometimes confused. Why is that? One we are humans and secondly, we believed that the individual would hold and live up to what they promised.

Being in a relationship it's a feeling of happiness, security, trust, and sense of protection. Let's stop playing it safe and dig deeper! Have you ever seen the movie *Love & Basketball*? Well, that is exactly how the relationship started. I was just a tomboy always playing rough, hanging with the boys and like a homie to the homeboys. Having a connection with someone who loved and played the same sport as you was amazing as a teenager. It wasn't long before the connection can be felt by those close to me. The homeboys were always like big brothers, so if you have a friendship or a brother like that you already know the comments and questions that were asked daily. As time continued, we found ourselves as best friends confiding in each other. We both came from slightly different walks of life but there were three things we had in common. Our biological fathers were drug users, our mothers were DEEP into church, and we both had stepfathers present in our lives. The conversations we had as teens when a parent would get on our nerves is what I believe allowed us to grow stronger together. We both never spoke to others regarding how we felt when it came to the adults responsible for raising us. To hear you act like or look like a person that you had no relationship never seen is by far too many mixed emotions for a child let alone a teenager trying to find their own identity.

We begin to talk on the phone for hours, skate together as a couple, crack jokes on each other and by all means swore we didn't like each other lol. At this point our trust to each other was a solid foundation to our friendship that no one could break.

December 17, 2002 was the day he asked me to be his girlfriend. I mean shoot, why not, with the connection we had. Again, just like the movie *Love & Basketball* we had a solid friendship before anything, and the connection of love was unexplainable. At our work Christmas party, it was obvious that we were a couple. That Christmas I visited family in St. Louis, Missouri-the Show Me State. I never felt such a loving, happiness in my life feeling. That was then the first time I've ever been in love.

As time went on, we went through some tough patches. I believed at the time love sometimes hurt and you just gotta work through it. No one in life is perfect but what I did not know or should I say realize. Love does not hurt and if someone loves you, they will not and I mean will not repeatedly hurt you. Yea the saying goes a person will only do what you allow. And what I allowed was repeated cheating, repeated disrespect, repeated being manipulated and repeatedly reminded of my weight. This treatment led me to a dark place a place where I then believed all the negative thoughts possible. The thought of the promises made and broken repeatedly. "I promise to never leave you, I promise to never hurt you again, - and the icing on the cake was, I promise to love you for you. The empty promises had me starting to question everything about myself and my purpose on earth.

Raising children alone there was no time to take a break from life to regroup. Nope not even a good night rest to feel a little ok. That is where I mastered putting on a mask daily. Yup that mask to cover and compress all of the hurt, guilt, embarrassment and the ugly person who I believed myself to be. This daily compression built itself from over time; day to day, week to week, and before I knew it, a year of complete darkness had gone by.

Let's take a break for a second and think about a few things. Do you see how I magically believe I was not worthy, valuable or even pretty enough to see who I really was? I allowed a repeated cycle to continue, allowed someone else's ignorance to make me blind. If you are currently in a dark place or know anyone in a dark place, simply encourage yourself or them daily. Tell yourself or them you are beautiful and wonderfully made just the way you are. And lastly love you for you!

After living in darkness for little over a year I began to accept life for what it is and make the necessary improvements for myself and kids. This was an everyday battle to better myself. At first, I could not look at myself in the mirror. Yes, I could look in the mirror. But what I am referring to is looking at the person in the mirror and accepting her for her.

On cloud 26, feels like the best moment of my life. Loving myself unconditionally, head held high, or can I just say I was feeling like I'm the shit. There was no stopping me I found myself and dared not to go back to that dark place. When you build yourself back together it's a little different than just picking yourself up.

Building yourself back together requires piece by piece analysis; determining what is meant to be versus what needs to be removed for the new you to flourish. In your mind and heart, you tell yourself *I will never allow anyone to break me again.*

Matter of fact anyone who breaks a promise, breaks their word, breaks their trust or breaks any boundaries will surely be dismissed- quick fast and in a hurry. When you get to this place in life you tend to guard yourself so much you begin to be- no, live in your purpose, passing up opportunities that are met you strengthen you let alone help someone else.

Let's take a break before this ride goes down the steep hill. Think for a second when you have been hurt. Do you change your ways based off of your emotions or off a clear mind that wants better? Yes, nine times out of ten changes are based off of emotions. It's okay. We've all been there or are currently residing there.

Building myself back to a place where I thought was best for me ended up putting me into a state of mind where I judged everyone who I felt was coming close to me. Not realizing I created the most unrealistic wall of protecting my heart from foolishness. Man, I tell you if never going to be hurt was a person it would be me, lol.

It took those who loved me dearly and those who I kept close to my heart to tell me who I was portraying was not truly me. I would hear "You gotta come out of that shell," or the famous line- "There is someone out there to just want to love you." My response for a period of time was, "I ain't going to be nobody's fool- trust me on that."

Someone should have brought out a cage and locked me in there because that's exactly how I built myself back, locking my heart in a cage and focusing on me.

I asked God a few times (God might say more than 1,000 times) what is wrong with me where did I go wrong am I pretty what do I need to do I'm listening God I just wanna be loved. As I began to look at myself all over again, I realized I fell back into depression. This time I fell fast just, like a roller coaster dropping at eighty miles per hour.

This time I was desperate to feel loved. I started going online looking for someone to validate me and see that

I am beautiful. What I actually found was a toxic person who only loved me for my appearance. You couldn't tell me anything, because once again I had a man! He told me EVERYTHING I wanted to hear. He once said, "I just wanted to have sex with you when I first seen you, but realized you were special." Clearly what he said it went right over my head and out the back door. Still having yet to deal with myself, f I just compressed that pain. When compressing hurt and pain it can be a very dangerous state of mind.

Before I knew it, I was facing all the hurt from the past. I faced it even more because I did not heal from the past trauma of heart break. Slowly but surely, I began to work on myself, but this time I kept God first. Truth be told there is no way possible to make it out of a dark place without Him. I spent a few months crying daily, angry with myself. However, I continued to press forward, determined to be the best version of myself.

Those promises that were made I understand now that you can not put all your trust into man. Anything can happen to change the current state, or the relationship NEVER held any value from the beginning. Just like a roller coaster ride, everything comes to a complete stop. That is exactly how I begun to truly heal. Everything must stop so that you can work yourself piece by piece. The process is not easy, but I promise you it is one hell of a feeling to be genuinely happy and at peace.

When it comes to a broken promise that hurt us, we may sometimes put ourselves through more heartache. What do I mean? Think about it, have you ever been told, "I promise to stay with you through thick or thin, good or bad, ups or downs" Then that individual decides to walk out of your life without a reason or explanation. We believed the promise that was made to us. When they walked out of our lives we question ourselves as to how they could leave you. In reality, their exit has NOTHING to do with you. See, that word promise sometimes is misused like the word love. Take a moment to reflect on that point.

As adults we did not experience a promise being broke through love as a teenager nor a young adult. A lot of times we base our experiences off of our young adult years instead of going to the beginning of where things originated.

As time goes on and we continue on our life journey we begin to pick up things that we know are not right, may hurt someone feelings, or change people's ways of thinking. We begin to make promises to people we love dearly and people who put their trust in us.

We all have made promises that were unable to keep. Regardless of the reason the promise is not being kept, someone trusted us and we failed them. We hurt them in some type of way. Some promises we were able to fulfill. Broken promises are something we should all take more seriously and not just make a promise because it seems right, sounds good, or we want to end the conversation when we feel our children are nagging us without reason.

As a parent I have probably broke more promises than a little bit with my kids. Not because I wanted to, but just maybe to satisfy them for the moment, not realizing how my actions effected their trust in me. So the next time you make a promise, hold yourself accountable or don't make it at all. The next time someone makes a promise to you, it is alright to tell them not to make the promise if they are unable to fulfill it.

Always remember, never be afraid of sharing your story because you just never know who you may help to overcome a situation in their own life.

Jeanetta Loveberry

Kiara

To every young lady who doesn't realize how strong you are, this chapter is dedicated to you. You are heard, seen and on the path to finding just what you need in life. No matter how hard the journey gets, keep going! You have no idea how close you are to your victory.

To my beautiful daughter, live and don't allow me or anyone else to stop you from being just who you are.

Destiny, continue paving your own path. Even when it seems uncertain, trust me you're doing amazing.

Khyra and Serenity, you girls show the world what you're made of. Nothing can stop you but you!

I've been where you all are currently. I may not know what you feel and why you're feeling it, but I know that with God you can get through anything and be the success YOU ALREADY ALL ARE. I LOVE YOU ALL TO LIFE!

Sincerely, Kiara

Broken but A Promise is a Promise
– Jeremiah 29:11

I can really say that starting off my life I had things all figured out. I knew exactly how I wanted my life to look what type of career I wanted, the house, the car, even down to the feeling of what I thought all that was supposed to bring.

And then I started to live.

I started to experience things and realize that life comes with so many ups and downs. From a young age, I realized that being let down was much more easier than being able to look forward to things. I started to transition from looking forward to these great things I had in mind to now not expecting much out of life. Taking situations for whatever they were became my motto. I started to accept what people would say about me, how they would treat me, the types of things that they would offer me as a person when it came to jobs or relationships and really their judgment about who I was as a person. What appeared to be well put together was slowly breaking inside.

I don't know exactly when my life took the shift from what seemed to be easy going to distressed. But what I can say is I remember a lot of bad about my childhood and not much good. I remember stories of hard times and trauma, but I always knew that it would be ok because that's just how things work with family. I'd like to believe that there are lots of great memories that seem to be clouded by memories that aren't the best. There were so many times I wanted to point the finger and say why things seemed so hard but soon as I thought of doing so, I realized that three more were pointing back at me. I never stepped up or spoke for myself. I knew what it was like to want so much out of life but feel like it's just not possible for me. To feel like so much good was happening but like I wasn't getting anywhere. So many people cheering me on, telling how much I've done over the years, when it felt like nothing to me. I didn't know how to celebrate my wins, often times not even thinking I was worthy of them.

Mental health concerns had taken a place in my life long before I knew what they were to acknowledge them. I always seemed to get by the radar like I had it together. Nobody knew I was suffering. My self-esteem was low, I had no direction in life, and I was getting by daily without actually feeling like I was living. On the outside, there were still others cheering me on and telling me just how great things were for me. I gave of myself when I had nothing to give. Often times feeling like making others feel full of themselves would some how reflect back on me.

That never worked!

All the giving that took place, NOBODY and I mean NOBODY stopped to ask me if I was ok or needed help. I just knew I was doing things for the greater good, or at least that's what I'd liked to tell myself. For years I struggled without, getting by on a hope and a prayer and the more I got by the more I lost myself. People pleasing was second nature to me and to feel the empowerment I felt from doing it saddens me to think about now but at the time I just knew I was saving the world. Not only was I lost but I was BROKEN!

How does life continue to go on when you feel like you're still trying to repair the little bit of life that you've been trying to scrounge up from a young age? That was a question I often asked myself, but had no answer. It was like I always knew in the end there would be a reward from the suffering. When the reward seems to never come by and the little that you thought you had left depleted, how do you continue on? I needed someone, anyone to come and rescue me from MYSELF! The thought that I had to fix things, the thought that if I just gave that someone would love and accept me, the thought that others would see beyond my dark skin or maybe just see that I was taking on so much so I wouldn't have to deal with life.

Well, there I was, three degrees in and I didn't know what was next. I had three jobs, went to school full time, and was a full-time mother. I was running, but burnout was chasing right behind me. I begin to feel like what once kept me motivated was becoming a burden. I struggled to do my daily routine- getting up at three in the morning, working a full day, caring for daughter, going to another job, then doing promotional work after, and doing schoolwork or having classes, finally getting to bed no earlier than eleven at night. For years that broken part of my story became normalized. Even then there were others who tried to help sporadically, but what I offered to give paled in comparison to the help I was offered. Not many people know what I experienced because I knew how to play the part. I knew to smile and brighten someone else's day even if I was having a rough one.

As much as I'd like to say that my teens and twenties were my hardest years, that did not compare to the brokenness of losing the very people you think will push you to go on forever. When I lost my grandmothers, it really hurt me, but to be honest I was able to press on a little because I had my grandfather who I thought the world of. We were alike in so many ways. He was a giver, he never really filled others with what was going on with him but took on their stuff and tried to help them make the best of it. He made sure even if he wasn't good that those around him always were. The very thing that made him who he was, was the very thing that ended his life… his heart. My pop pop had the biggest heart ever. When he left this earth, it broke my heart terribly. I always knew what it felt like to feel broken, but this level of broken had been something I'd never experienced. I wanted him back to show me in action not just words what it meant to be a man, to love and cherish others and to be my biggest cheerleader even when I didn't know how to cheer for myself.

Brokenness finally revealed a deep depression.

For so many years I was able to live in my brokenness covering it with various things. When my grandfather died, I was forced to face my brokenness. It knocked me down, made me question life and often times left me feeling like everything was so unfair. In that brokenness I had to move on without my grandparents and I wasn't sure how to. I tried counseling, prayer, and church; hoping and sometimes screaming for God to help me understand. During a hard time when the world was not as fast paced, I was forced to deal with brokenness.

There are still days when I face challenges, but I can say that when I started to put in the work for myself things begin to turn around. I started speaking the word back to myself. The promises God gave me haven't failed, I failed to stay the course. So, in that broken place I had to embrace what was and work through that. Believe me, as I continue to do the work nothing about it is easy.

As I reflect back on life and all I've been through I often felt like a lot of people just didn't get me. My current therapist summed up my life for me during one session and he probably doesn't know it. His words hit hard when he said something along the lines of "Kiara, you know how to weather a storm, so you sit back and wait for whatever that's going to happen to just happen." For the first time I finally felt like someone got it! Like I was finally heard!

God knows what we need and when we need it. I could probably go on and on about the way things could've, should've worked out for me but right when I was at my very end that's when hope was restored again. Not that it hadn't happened in other instances but that was a turning point I needed to go from broken to being repaired.

Dear ME,

I write to you publicly as I lost you privately. You have lived this beautifully broken life for far too long. There's so much I wish you knew at a younger age, so much trauma I wish I could've protected you from. But I must say that in the face of adversity you've shown up and conquered even when you didn't feel like you deserved an applause. Reflecting on my journals, the thoughts that often times swarmed my mind and all that you've been through, it hasn't been the easiest, but you've always tried your best.

I write you to let you know that no good thing will be withheld from you. You are the author of this story with God's direction and one day you're going to be extremely proud. No more will you have to give without receiving. You are a gift that God cherishes.

Continue to love yourself harder, be aware of your emotions and don't avoid them. As you are learning never forget to teach. There are a lot of young ladies that need to hear from you, so release the fear and go out there and help others get through what seemed like impossible to you. Be your authentic self and remember that your story has shaped an amazing individual. You have the support, utilize it. One last thing: YOU ARE ENOUGH, YOU ARE

WORTHY AND EVEN BROKEN CRAYONS CREATE BEAUTIFUL PORTRAITS!

-Kiara

Tureka

Broken Promises
True to Self

We make promises to ourselves, and we break them, at least I did several times. Whether small or large, life changing or not, a promise is a promise and promises should be kept. Nineteen years ago, I broke a promise to myself. Today, I am holding firm and maintaining my promise.

My girlfriend told me about a book called <u>Satan I am Taking My Health Back</u>. I purchased the book. I was on a journey of vegetarianism and self-healing of my mind, body and soul. I was broken, beat down, full of pain, tired of rejection, tired of feeling like a failure and making bad decisions. I was functioning and taking care of business. From the outside looking in people thought I was doing well. I appeared to have it all figured out. Honestly, I did not, it was a mask that I wore every single day fooling everyone around me and deep down inside I was broken into a million little pieces. I wanted everything in my life to be better, I was not satisfied with the limitations, I wanted happiness, blissfulness, peace and calm. My grandmother Glo always said that life is what you make it. So, I promised myself that I would make life everything I wanted it to be for ME. I started making small changes in my diet, exercising more, meditation and trying to live stress free. At the time I was a single parent of a premature newborn. I blamed myself for this, I felt that it was my fault and lack of self-care that led to me having my son two months prematurely. I did not know the direction my life was going in and I wanted a change. I promised myself that I would focus on being a better person, living a better life, eating better, quieting my mind, and living stress free. I did not want the stress and pressures of life plaguing my soul. I did not like the way I felt, I was willing to do anything in my power to change that. I started out on a great path but slowly, I broke that promise to myself.

Life gets in the way. You set goals, and things will happen to derail you off your path. Some things are unforeseen and beyond our control and some things are not. I allowed a failed marriage to stand in the way of keeping my promise to myself. I allowed lack of employment to stand in the way of keeping my promise to myself. I allowed societal goals to stand in the way of keeping my promise to myself. I allowed the death of a loved one to stand in the way of keeping my promise to myself. I allowed illness to stand in the way of keeping my promise to myself. I allowed the unforeseen circumstances of dealing with everyday life to stand in the way of keeping my promise to myself. I can use all the excuses in the world but at the end of the day, it was a lack of self-love and determination that stood in the way of keeping my promise to myself. I realized that I did NOT love myself. I lost my drive, I lost my will and I was unable to maintain my promise and my goals.

Making sure you reassure and reaffirm to yourself to maintain your promises and goals. It is easier said than done. It is hard to maintain when everything around you is crumbling. It is hard to maintain when it seems like the world is against you. It is hard but it does not have to stay hard. Now I realize that fact and every day I make sure that I maintain my sanity and maintain my promise to myself. At the end of the day there is nothing more important than MYSELF. If I am not 100% and on my "A" game, I cannot be a great mother, a great employee, a great friend and just a great all-around human being. A failed marriage, career derailment, uprooting and moving to another state, threw me from my game. I fell and I got back up, I fell harder but I did not allow those obstacles to destroy me and the mission I had set forth for my life. It paused the operation, but it did not stop the progression. The loss of my grandmother changed my world forever. She died suddenly; it was a blow that no one in my family expected. She was our Matriarch and was supposed to live to be one hundred years old- not die at sixty-seven. How could this be, how could this happen? Two weeks before her passing, I found out that I was pregnant with my second child. After her funeral, as I tried to get my life on track and prepare for the bundle of joy I was going to deliver, I was laid off from work. His father and I broke up. No problem, I thought. This is what he and I do. We've participated in a cycle of break ups and reconciliation for twenty-five years. Little did I know, the stress of it had taken a toll on me. I will never forget going to get an ultrasound and the doctor came in to talk to me. He said that I was already dilated three centimeters and the only way to carry my baby to term was to get a cervical cerclage. "Huh?" was my response, as it all sounded like gibberish to me.

"What does that mean? Well, now you are on bed rest for the rest of your pregnancy, you must get weekly shots and weekly ultrasounds," was the response. Not to mention the other obstacle, the fact that I was what they called advanced maternal age.

This is not the end of the world. I am a fighter, I will get past this; I will win. I delivered a healthy baby thankfully. The level of depression I experienced took a toll on my son, my mom and my body. Over the next three years, the blows kept coming in my direction, I was diagnosed with thyroid cancer, my son was diagnosed with autism, I went through another divorce and every promise that I made to myself years ago, I literally broke. I allowed myself to be the broken, beat down, full of pain, tired of rejection, tired of feeling like a failure and the bad decision-making person I was in the past. One would think with a cancer diagnosis that you would do everything you can to maintain your health. I did the best I could at the time, I followed the doctor's orders. I could have done more for myself. I ate well but my focus was on my kids. I was still trying to pull myself out of the depression that kept me bound.

After my second divorce and moving into my new house, I realized that I needed to get back on track. I was maintaining but I wasn't living, I wasn't thriving as I should. I wasn't the example of a human being that I wanted my kids to see. I was broken. I decided that enough was enough. I remembered how I promised myself to take care of myself. I promised myself that I would focus on being a better person, living a better life, eating better and quieting my mind. I promised myself that I would not be stressed out and let the pressures of life plague my soul. I started to build myself up one day at a time.

I started getting back to the things that I did in the past, walking, sitting at the beach, hiking, meditating, exercising, yoga, and reading self-help books. I immersed myself into healing. I added EFT tapping, mirror exercises, followed the medical medium, and listened to affirmations. I was seeing a therapist, I listened to every positive message I could find, Sadguru, David Goggins, Iyanla Vansant, Joe Dispenza, Louise Hay, Miles Monroe, Michael Singer etc. I brought books and pulled out every little nugget of information I thought would benefit me. I had supportive people by my side, and I am truly thankful for them. I also had to remove some people from my life who were unhealthy for my well-being. I had several crying sessions alone in the dark, I cried myself to sleep many nights. I have faced my fears, faced my demons, and I faced MYSELF. I allowed myself to heal from my past, I let go of mistakes, failures and pain. The one thing that I realized through my journey here on this earth is that I did NOT love myself. It was extremely hard to admit. Even harder to look myself in the mirror and face the person I allowed myself to become. I wasn't whole, I wasn't happy, I wasn't me. Thankfully, that is in the past. I have my grandmother Glo's favorite words on replay in my head. "Keep The FAITH". That keeps me going. I am proud to say that today I am the person that I want to be. I am not perfect, it has been a battle, but I am a VICTOR. I am healthy, my kids are healthy, my career surpassed my expectations, most importantly I LOVE MYSELF, I am gentle with myself. I look back at the promises I made in the past and I have exceeded my expectations and more. I matured, I realized what matters in life, and started to appreciate life. I live a life of peace. I will never break another promise to myself because I realize how important I am, I know my worth. I have a place here on earth, I was put here for a reason, I am worthy, and I will continue to be a quality human being to others while loving myself and appreciating every breath that I breathe.

-Tureka

Lauren

Relationship Addict

I've spent so many years trying to fill this void with relationships, and sex all because I didn't want to be alone. I spent most of my life trying to please others in fear of rejection and abandonment. The happiness of others was top priority, causing me to neglect myself and my needs. I was content with putting myself on the back burner and wearing myself out so I could see others be happy and prosperous. I was this way with family, friends and my relationships.

I thought that if you showered them with love, gifts, and undivided attention, it would keep them around. I learned over the years that it only kept them around because they benefited from you. I did all of this because I was afraid to be alone. My relationship with my family was the root problem of all of my trust and abandonment issues over the years. This would cause me to be clingy, anxious, and insecure.

I often found myself in situations where I wasn't happy, but to say I was in a relationship was all I wanted. I would fall in love with the person's passion and potential, not their current state. I didn't care what you were passionate about as long as you were happy, I was happy. I was constantly in situations where I was mentally broken all of the time.

The first relationship that ruined my trust was when I was twenty-seven. Everything was good at first. He wined and dined me all the time, but eventually the relationship took a turn for the worse. I dealt with cheating multiple times, emotional and physical abuse, and I lost two babies behind this relationship. I stayed with this man for four years and dealt with the abuse and neglect. I stayed around while he cheated and spent my money on other women because I was afraid to leave him.

Once I ended the relationship, I trusted no one but I still had the urge to be with someone. I started to fill this void with meaningless relationships, doing whatever I could. I felt meaningless, like I had no one. All of my friends were living their lives, getting married, having children and here I was- alone.

I started having relationships that would last anywhere from six months to two years and the cycle would start again. I was too clingy, anxious, and insecure. I was still carrying baggage from my previous relationship, expecting them to help me unpack. It was so hard trusting again and being secure with myself that it caused multiple problems and I would get cheated on again. I left every relationship crying, depressed, and blaming myself.

When I started any new relationship, I was their go to person for anything they needed. My goal was to keep him happy so he wouldn't leave me. All my actions actually did was show how easy and gullible I was. I've met some good men, that would've given me the world but I was stuck those who neglected and mistreated me. I finally realized that I was looking for the love that I yearned for as a child. I was missing out on something that caused me to constantly try to fill a void.

Whenever I thought there was some light at the end of the tunnel, something else would happen. Situations like money being stolen from me, a phone call from another woman letting me know that she's been sleeping with him, or the abuse. It made me feel like the scum of the earth. *Here I am once again looking like a fool because I gave my all to this man only to find out that he was using me or he just didn't care.* I would think to myself each and every time.

So, here I am again with even more baggage, begging for love and affection. I would constantly trick myself into thinking that he loves me and he's just too busy at the moment, or he has a lot going on. I had to stop lying to myself and others. I had enough of everything, and I had to run away.

After years of failed relationships, I decided to pack up and move my family to Tennessee, expecting change. I met someone who was just like me, insecure, anxious and clingy, I finally had a mirror placed in front of me and I saw who I really was. The roles reversed, I took advantage and mistreated him. I became the type of person I was trying to avoid. After that relationship, I gave up, not only on myself but those close to me. I accepted the fact that I would never get married or have a meaningful relationship, ever.

A year after I ended this relationship, I met someone that was established, kind and caring. Little did I know, he was emotionally constipated. His business came before our relationship, and I once again was alone.

He would take me on trips, out to dinner, and sometimes help me with my bills, but that wasn't what I needed. I needed someone to love me the way loved them. I would express to him how I felt, and he would cut off all communication with me for days until he felt like talking with me. I gathered up the strength to walk away and figure out what I need to do with myself and how to heal myself. I left Tennessee heartbroken, sad, alone, and still feeling worthless, on the tail of another failed relationship.

After moving back to Delaware, I had another bad relationship and finally realized that I needed help. I was dating an older man who I thought would treat me better since he was more experienced. He ended up being a professional narcissist who was good with gaslighting, love bombing and lying. I fell for his tricks every time he opened his mouth. I was happy at first, then miserable. Yet, I never left because I was scared to be by myself. Finally, I had enough of the lies, cheating, fighting over finances and his refusal to take any accountability, so I left. I needed therapy again. I had to stop blaming others for the vicious cycle. I had to set an example for my son regarding how women should be respected and treated. Also, I needed to be an example to show how we as women had to practice self-love and care. I've been in therapy for almost two years now. I set boundaries, I pray, and most of all, I love myself.

I endured bruises, miscarriages, abortions, anger,

fear, neglect, and verbal abuse to say I was in a relationship. I was tired of anxiety, depression, and feeling worthless. We can only change ourselves when we are ready, and once we change, others will see the impact. Allowing these things to happen in relationships only breaks us down and makes us settle for less of what we deserve. We can't blame everything on the other person in the relationship, we must take accountability for what we're not doing or what we continue to put up with. Loving ourselves first will open our eyes to what we deserve as well as what should not be tolerated in every aspect of life.

-Lauren

Dara

Trust in God's Promise

What do the terms promises, brokenness, and brokenness in biblical terms mean? Well... you will see, while you go on a journey with me through one aspect of my life and how the title of my chapter ties together.

PROMISES: I do my best to keep any promises I make to someone, or to myself. Webster's dictionary defines the term promise as: *A declaration that one will do or refrain from doing something specific.*

To me, keeping a promise has to do with keeping your word or expectations for yourself or of someone. You don't necessarily have to use the term specifically, in order to break one. Between the ages of four and five, I already had made my first promise to myself.

Hollywood, California 1977-1978. Lots of sunshine, beaches and palm trees. Here is where I remember my first memory of life. I was between the ages of four and five. My family and I lived off of Sunset and Bronson St. In a two-bedroom apartment. I lived with my mom, my older sister and a man I considered my dad. My biological father lived nearby in Compton. I remember being a shy, but an active little girl, who loved to talk, daydream and thought the world and the people in it was a beautiful place. I was a happy go lucky kid. Things were perfect to me. That all changed one night. I recall sitting on the couch one evening watching TV. I'm not sure how the altercation started between my parents, but I do remember they were in their room. The next thing you know, my dad was dragging my mom into the living room, and he was hitting her. I immediately started screaming and crying, not knowing what was going on. My mom was crying and yelling, and I didn't know what to do. My older sister went into our room and came back out with the bed post from our bed and said, "I dare you to hit her again!" she threatened to hit him with the bed post if he struck my mom one more time. The police were called, and they took my dad away. He was gone for a couple of days and returned beating and banging on the door, saying he was sorry and begging my mom to let him in. I was terrified because I wasn't sure if my mom believed him or not. I didn't want her to let him in due to how traumatized I was a couple of nights ago. I can't say that this type of behavior happened a lot in my presence after that night, but it only took that one time for me to make a promise to myself that I would never let a man put his hands on me like that. I would never allow a man to disrespect me or try to control me. I should have not been subjected to even making promises like that at a young age.

There are numerous definitions for the terms broken and brokenness. Webster's dictionary defines each as follows-

Broken: *2.(of a person) having given up all hope; despairing.*

Brokenness: *3. Having been violated; a broken promise.*

Growing up primarily in single parent household with my mother, there were plenty of times I felt hopeless and broken based off the way I was raised, but I was able to bounce back with no problem. During my adolescent years I made lots of promises to myself not only about how I wanted to be treated by a man, but also how I would raise my kids and the structure of how I thought my life would go. I'm the type of person who always has a reason or explanation for every action in my life. For the first time in my life at the mere age of 21, I was speechless, motionless, confused, angry, distraught and in shock. I questioned who I was, my faith, and God. That's what broken/brokenness felt like for me.

1994 San Diego, California: I was 21 years old and had just graduated from San Diego Job Corps from the H.O.T. (Health Occupational Training program), as a CNA. I was super stoked because I had my foot in the door in the medical field. I decided to move back to Delaware. I really missed my family and friends. Returning home, I had goals to concentrate on finding a job and eventually furthering my career in healthcare. This meant I had no time for a relationship. That too was a promise I made to myself before I left California! I eventually found a job and was looking into taking courses in athletic training. Life was grand and everything was going well. Running errands with my sister one day, I ran into a man who would later on be the father of my first- born child. Of course at the time, he was just a stranger making audible noises trying to talk to me. Walking past his car, he started talking to me. We exchanged numbers, but I really didn't think anything of it. It didn't take him that long to call me. Our first conversation we found out that we both liked the same sports team, our birthdays were in July, and we liked basketball. Now I only knew him for three months before my life did a complete one hundred and eighty degree turn. During those three months we had three planned outings. Our first one was shooting hoops. The second outing was eating lunch at Boston Market and our third outing was shooting pool at the bar downstairs below his barber shop on Market St. In between those outings, we spoke on the phone a couple of times. I visited his barber shop and went to his house a few times. As far as I was concerned, he was just a cool guy to hang out with every now and then. At some point he did ask me about wanting to date. I was a little taken back by his statement because there was nothing romantically going on between us. I quickly told him NO! I explained to him that I didn't come back home to jump into a relationship. Focusing on my goals was my number one priority and I didn't want any distractions. I told him we can be friends. I want to focus on my future before I even think about being with some man. Besides talking to him was all about him. I have never met someone so into themselves. I could never be with someone like that. I remember being at his house one day and him telling me that he wanted to me to have his baby. I said, "You have two kids that you don't take care of now, what do I look like having your baby, plus we're not dating or anything. We're just friends!" He went on to say how beautiful our baby would be if we had a girl and she had my big eyes and dimples, as if I hadn't expressed the exact opposite of his statement. He totally ignored me. As I was about to leave, he asked if I wanted to come back later that night to hang out and listen to music. I was hesitant because I had never been to his house when it was dark outside. I told him I guess I could. A few hours later I returned, and we were sitting on the floor listening to music. The next thing I know he was trying to wrestle with me. Being a tom-boy I wrestled with a lot of guys, but I just wasn't in the mood to do so. I told him I needed to use the bathroom. He said, "No you don't, you're going to leave." I replied, stating that I really had to use the bathroom. Although I did want to leave, I promised I would come back. That was one promise I wish I broke! Little did I know going back down those stairs would change my life. Upon entering his room, he was sitting on his bed and motioned for me to sit next to him. I said, "No!" I didn't want him to try and wrestle with me again. He said he was not going to do anything, but I still said, "No, I'm good!" He then promised me that he wasn't going to do anything, so I trusted him and complied. We laid there and listened to music. After some time passed, the tables turned. He turned over to try and kiss me and I resisted. In a blink of an eye, he was on top of me and pinned my hands above my head. I tried my hardest to move my hands, but the way he had them, I was unable to move. I immediately crossed my legs to try and protect myself down there. He used his knees and one hand to get my pants down far enough (not all the way) and pry my legs open and forced himself in me. For the first time in my life, I felt completely

POWERLESS! I was in such a state of shock once he was done, I felt paralyzed. I couldn't even muster up any energy to even scream. I was trying to process what just happened. I'm a strong girl, but the tactics that he used, made me believe this was not the first time this man has done this. While I was trying to take in what happened, he had the nerve to rub my belly and say, "Now you're going to have my baby," without a care in the world about what he just did. Once I recovered from my state of shock, I got up and left. I walked to my car, and I just sat there. I didn't even start the car. I was too busy contemplating if I should go to the police or to the hospital so they could do a rape exam. Before I could even make a decision on what to do, my brain flooded with a bunch of thoughts. If I went to the police, what type of questions would they ask? Would they ask me questions as if I asked for it? I mean I was fully dressed from head to toe. As a tomboy, I didn't dress provocatively. Would they question me on why I was over there at night and if we were dating? I eventually talked myself out of going to the police. On to the next...the hospital. If I went there and tell them what transpired, they would definitely call the police! I sat in my car for a good ten minutes or so before I decided I was just going to go home and forget it happened. I didn't think anyone would have believed me. Why would he do this to me? Not once did I ever flirt with him. Why didn't I just leave after I went to the bathroom? Why do you trust people so much? After all these questions had bombarded my brain, I started my car and drove home. I went upstairs and took a shower. Once I was done getting ready to lay down, I looked at my calendar to see what the date was. It was June 5th, 1995. I went to bed and never spoke a word about what happened to me to anyone.

Meaning of Brokenness found in the Bible: Being broken is a gift because when we are broken, the need for a savior is recognized in order to make us whole. A broken heart is one that is open to Him, that lets in grace. Brokenness in God's eyes is being so crushed by the sin and darkness of the world that we know there is no place to turn but to God!

Not too long after I was raped, this man kept calling my house. If I answered the phone, I would hang up on him. If my sister answered the phone, I would tell her to tell him I wasn't there! A couple of weeks went by and I felt I was finally able to put the situation to rest because he stopped calling. After about a month my stomach started cramping. I figured my period was about to start. The cramping went on for a couple of weeks and I kept checking to see if my period had appeared. I was so conflicted on why I kept cramping, but Aunt Flow wasn't showing up. I really didn't keep track of my period because I wasn't sexually active. I remembered my last period was towards the end of May. I checked my calendar to see how long it had actually been since my last period. I then sat on the edge of the bed in my sister's room pondering on what was going on with my cycle. I just couldn't understand why I kept cramping, but not bleeding. Out of nowhere my brain did a rewind like a VCR tape and I yelled out the name of the man who raped me. In that short amount of time, I guess I suppressed what had happened. I ran to my calendar and counted the days again. Then I made a mad dash to Rite-Aid to get a pregnancy test. I took the test as soon as I got home, but I couldn't tell if I was actually pregnant or not. The line was faint, and I was around the twenty-eight day mark. So, I decided to wait the full thirty days. That Friday, I went and bought another test and took it again. Sure enough, clear as day, it was POSITIVE. I left the test on the bed and called my mom at work and told her. She asked me if I was going to marry him? At this point, I still hadn't told anyone what happened on June 5th. My response to her question was probably not what she was expecting.

I told her...HELL NO! I didn't feel comfortable telling her why because we didn't have that type of relationship. I felt she always found me at fault with things, so I wasn't even going to go down that road with her. My younger sister came home with a friend and unfortunately, I had left the test on my sister's bed. She came down the hall asking who was pregnant? Her friend said she would go with me to Planned Parenthood because I didn't know where it was. But before I went, I drove to his job to show him the pregnancy test and when he looked at it... HE SMILED. Then he said, "How do you know for sure?" I said that's why I'm going to the doctors to make sure and I drove off. The doctor at Planned Parenthood confirmed that I was indeed pregnant and told me my due date was February 28th, based off of when I thought my last period was.
Now I've always said, if I was ever raped that would be

the only time I would get an abortion. I couldn't imagine raising or loving a kid out of a violent act. I didn't want to be reminded of it. Once I was done speaking to the doctor, I went into a room to talk to a counselor. I guess it was protocol. We sat down and she basically went over my options. I didn't tell her how I got pregnant either. I just shared I was thinking about getting an abortion, but I was uncertain for sure. I never thought in this moment, it would be so hard to make a decision that in theory, my mind had already been made up to do. My brain was on board for an abortion, but my heart was telling me something else. I was so conflicted that I really had to give it some time to make sure I was making the right decision. I knew when the cutoff date was to have an abortion, so I took my time since I was uncertain. As time went by, I reached out to my rapist and told him I was for sure pregnant. I was still torn on what to do. I was still leaning to getting an abortion and it was getting closer to that time to make a decision. Why is this so hard to decide, I kept asking myself? You never know what you're going to do about a situation until you are in that situation. Growing up in church and having my Grandmother talk to me about God all the time is how I started having faith in God as a child. I recall hearing about going into your prayer closet when you need an answer from God. At this point in my life, I needed God to help me with this decision. I was so broken about this I could hardly breathe.

This act of indecisiveness weighed so heavily on my heart. I needed to act and act fast. I wanted to try this

prayer closet that I heard so much about, but our closets were too small to go in. I went to our back room and sat on the corner of our pull-out couch. I sat in silence but internally I was going off in my head. Yelling at God in an outrage and asking him, *"Why would you allow this to happen to me?"* Most importantly, *"Why would you allow me to get pregnant. I'm mad at you for this. I know I'm not a virgin. I had sex before and the one time I didn't consent I was raped and end up pregnant? God, are you punishing me? I thought you were my protector. I only have a few weeks to make up my mind. Keeping this baby goes against every promise I made to myself about having kids by different dads, out of wedlock, being a single mom and struggling, I didn't want to repeat the patterns in my family. I wanted to be well established first. This was not how I planned my life!"*
After venting to God about all the emotions that were bottled up inside me, my mind was clear, and I was calm and it was very quiet in the room. Out of nowhere I heard this soft, subtle, calming voice whisper...*TRUST ME!*
I said, "What?"
I heard it again...*TRUST ME!*
I said... "TRUST YOU?" I spoke back and said," I've trusted you and had faith in you and look where I'm at now!
Once again that calming voice reiterated *TRUST ME!* I said, "OK God, I will trust you." I got up from the bed with my mind made up and just before I opened the door I told God, "I don't know what your plan is, but I'm going to trust you again." Although I said I would trust Him, I was still afraid of the unknown and I still

didn't want to be a single mom.

Six months went by, and I hadn't spoken to the father of my baby since I decided to keep it, or to let him know I was leaving the state. Before I found out that I was pregnant my sister (best friend) from California, called to tell me she was pregnant. A few weeks later, I called her to tell her I was too. Neither one of us were going to be with the father of our child, so I asked her to ask mom if I can move back out there so we could raise our kids together. My doctor told me I couldn't fly past seven months. As I was making arrangements to leave, I started getting phone calls again from you know who. I was still hanging up on him and not willing to talk. After numerous calls from him, I finally talked to him and asked him what he wanted. He said he wanted to talk to me and if he could pick me up. I gave him the okay hoping this will be the last time he contacted me. When he arrived, we took a short drive to get gas. I didn't have anything to say, and he was quiet too. How stupid could I be to agree to this. I was having second thoughts, but it was too late, I was already in the car. I kept my hand on the door handle in case I need to make a quick exit. He caught me off guard once and that wasn't going to happen again. Because it was so quiet on the way back to my house, I finally said, "What do you want to talk about?" By this time, we were parked in front of my house. He proceeded to tell me he didn't want me to move to California. He wanted me to stay here, marry him and get our own place. I actually chuckled out of anger and asked him, "Why would I stay here, marry you and live with you?" I yelled... "YOU

VIOLATED MY BODY!"

This narcissistic man had the audacity to say, "I did it on purpose to keep you."

I was so taken back by what he said. All I could say was, "You never had me, and I guess your plan didn't work." I got out of the car and slammed the door. I was livid! Within the next three weeks, I got prepared to move back to California.

December 5, 1995: I made it to California safely. Being six and a half months pregnant, I didn't even bother looking for a job. Instead, my mom dropped me off at the welfare office to apply for assistance. Here I was visiting those thoughts again about how this was not supposed to be my life. But I knew it was temporary. For the next month and a half, I really didn't do much but prepare to have this baby. Before I left Delaware, I had my anatomy ultrasound done. My due date changed from February 28th to March 10th. During my ultrasound the tech asked if I wanted to know the gender of the baby and I declined. I wanted to be surprised but I also didn't care. I had this gut feeling that I was having a girl. I thought of a couple of names for both genders but wasn't sold on any name other than "Jaide" as a middle name for a girl. One day watching a talk show on TV. There was this little girl named "Promise." I loved her name. I kept staring at it every time it showed up on the screen. My spirit was telling me if I had a girl, this should be her name. I went down memory lane about all the promises I made to myself on how I wanted to raise my kids and how I wanted to be the first to break generational curses in my family. That name would have great meaning behind it and a reminder of the type of parent I want to be. Kind of like God giving us the rainbow as a promise, to remind himself that he wouldn't destroy the earth by water again. Promises to me means love, protection, being consistent, and never giving up!

On **February 26, 1996**, a Monday morning, I went into labor at thirty-eight weeks. I was not ready for this day at all. I was super nervous being this was my first baby, and I had no clue what to expect. Even though I had my second family there with me for support, I still felt alone. By no means did I ever picture myself bringing a human being into this world under these circumstances. I saw myself as another stereotypical black woman. How would I afford to take care of this baby? How would we survive? I had barely scratched the surface of my career. No husband, no savings, no place of my own. Six months ago, I said I would trust in God's answer and there was no turning back now. As my baby came down the birth canal and took its first breath, I was relieved that it was over. I was so done; I didn't even ask what the gender was. My sister asked and the doctor told us…a girl! My little Promise, a gift from God was born.

My daughter is 26 years old now. I have two beautiful granddaughters! Over those 26 years of her life, I was worried about all the promises I made and broke. The fears and what ifs that I was deeply concerned about never transpired. By the time Promise was a teenager

I had been married for seven years and she had a younger brother, it finally dawned on me why God said to trust Him. I worked one to two jobs during the first six years of Promise's life. I worked graveyard shift as a CNA and a part-time position as a teacher for preschool/pre-K school-age children. I never paid the school for bringing Promise to work with me. I had free babysitters. I never ended up on welfare. I didn't struggle as much as I thought I would. In that moment of this random thought, I was able to see how truly blessed I was. My kids grew up in a two-parent home with lots of love, affirmations, discipline, laughter, encouragement, and so on. Although we weren't rich or perfect parents, and there were struggles, we had family values. That was one of the promises I kept. God knew his plan for me when I didn't. I didn't understand what he meant by saying, "Trust me!" If there is anything you can gain from my testimony, just know that you're stronger than you think you are. Trust in God when he speaks to you!

-Dara

Janie

Forever Tanya

October 24, 1994 -I just got hired at MBNA, a very prestigious bank. My starting salary was a whopping six dollars per hour, working in the mail room. I actually liked the challenge of operating the machines and maneuvering from one task to the next. Little did I know that this job would force my heart to open and allow God to truly speak to me; and for me to listen intently without fear of being wrong.

My story is about my nineteen-year-old daughter Tanya. I was working all night, getting good at my career while she watched her younger siblings. I had three younger girls whom she adored. Tanya was my help and my best friend.

One day she came to me and said, "Mom, there is this lump on my neck." This was about two weeks after I'd started work. She had just been removed from my insurance due to her age. I took her to the emergency room, thinking *this is an easy fix*. It didn't hurt to the touch, and she only complained about the heart burn. I bought her some antacids and she always felt better. But this lump was new and unusual.

"Come on baby, this shouldn't take long." She was fine with whatever I said. She trusted me and I trusted the hospital to fix this.

Walking through the doors I'd taken for granted the possibility of this being a small hiccup and the doctors had the answer. I wasn't prepared for the journey I was about to embark.

She was seen right away. The doctor felt the lump and immediately ordered x-rays. I said, "What is it?"

He smiled and said, "Not too much to worry about. Let's see what the x-ray shows."

"Ok I'm with that," I replied.

Tanya watched me as I maintained a calm face, as I just knew it was nothing. She was my comfort and my strength. I figured we would be in and out with some meds to shrink whatever the lump turned out to be.

She wasn't worried and I wasn't either, until the doctor returned with a second doctor as well as the x-ray results in his hand. Hanging them on the screen I could sense he was about to tell me something I wouldn't understand, but he just kept a calm face and said, "She has a growth in her chest, and we can shrink it with medicine."

"A growth, what kind of growth and where did it start.?" I questioned.

He stated, "There is nothing to worry about, we can fix this with a few treatments. She will be fine, no need to worry."

The second doctor stood motionless and said nothing.

Tanya was watching my face and I was looking at the doctor. He seemed confident that this was nothing.

He again promised this was nothing to worry about and she would be fine. He told me she would need a biopsy and soon so they could start treatment. They didn't tell me where to look or how to find this doctor without the great Medicaid. My baby was no longer covered by my insurance, and I had no idea how to handle this.

The next day I called the hospital for information regarding how to go forward with the doctor's order for a biopsy and treatment. I was getting worried, but I didn't allow my mind to fall into doubt land. If I did that it would be like I gave into fear. I began the calls, getting prepared to stop only when I accomplished my goal. I was not taking no for an answer. I kept calling and getting switched to other numbers, sometimes getting the same person over and over. Finally, I broke down making sure I was out of ear shot of Tanya. My exact words were, "Stop sending me thru changes! I need a doctor to do a biopsy so I can get help for my daughter. PLEASE HELP ME!" Well, what do you know, that worked. The person on the other end of the call took my charge and didn't leave me. I wish I knew her name, but she stayed on the line with me until we found a doctor that would see Tanya, providing care without insurance. Wow...my first encounter with an angel.

The doctor was in a fancy suite with a beautiful office. It was no welfare office. This was a private practice, and he was so nice and welcoming.

After speaking to us in his professional yet friendly manner he assured us that this was something he could bill me for. *Wow who does this*, I thought, but his warm smile soon assured me we were in good hands.

Tanya was scheduled to have the biopsy done on November 12, 1994. She had to be at the hospital by 6:00 a.m. I was excited to get this over with. Tanya and I were in this together, but God had his hand all up and through the situation. We were never alone- even if I thought we were.

The procedure went well, and we went home. Hugging her and assuring her this was the beginning, and we would walk the journey together.

I kept working as usual and not taking this thing seriously. How crazy was I? Life is not to be taken for granted EVER!!!!

It didn't take long for the results to come in. I was at work and my mother called. She said the doctor called and told her the results of the biopsy. What she said next didn't hit me at first because I didn't know what this was.

She told me in a comforting voice that to me, said everything is fine, that the doctor said she has Hodgkin's Lymphoma. Even though I heard the results, at the time I did not know what that diagnosis meant. My ignorance led me to make a few phone calls to different offices or nurses- anyone who would listen.

I asked them to explain what a Hodgkin's Lymphoma was. With each call, the answer was always the same- it is a form of cancer. No one would tell me for sure what that meant. In my mental blur, it never occurred to me to ask the doctor who gave the diagnosis. Crazy me.

By this time, I was numb. I couldn't think. I remember walking back to my desk and putting my head down to absorb the information. I kept thinking, this is not a cold, this is not a chest pain, and this is not something I can cure at home. What... what is this? I'm telling you I was a lost mother with no answers. I put my head in my hands and finally cried. I didn't know what to do with the information regarding my daughter's diagnosis. Cancer was not an easy fix- I knew that much!

Suddenly, thru my tears, I felt warm and held, it was as if I was surrounded by a cloud of pure love. Never had I felt anything like this comforting touch. However what happened next, I would never forget. I heard a voice so loud and clear, it took me by surprise. The voice was strong yet gentle, and like my father was interrupting my pain to relay a message. The voice said so plainly. *"Don't cry my baby, I am taking my child home. You will be fine, but she has to come home."* I lifted my head to look around, I thought I was imagining things. Like yeah right- God is talking to me directly. No preacher or psychic. What I heard was the real deal, even though I still didn't trust or believe it. I told two or three friends of mine what happened, and they listened without criticizing. I kind of left the experience hanging in those conversations and focused on caring for my Tanya.

The next events were nothing short of miracles. My baby didn't believe in TMH [The Most High] nor did I. I see now He had to knock me down to pick me back up by His grace. If I only believed when He said He was taking her home, I would have never put her through fourteen sessions of horrible chemo. Chemo is short for chemotherapy. Eventually, I discovered that chemotherapy is actually chemical therapy used to treat cancer. During chemo, approximately nine different chemicals would go into her veins to slowly destroy the bad, cancerous cells. Unfortunately, in the process, good cells would also be destroyed, but the treatment was deemed necessary by her physician to treat her.

I finally talked to the doctor who explained she would need a port in her chest to administer the chemo. The same wonderful doctor also did the procedure. It was the same time in the morning and the same confident smile from him reassuring me that everything was going to be fine. She had to get in touch with an oncologist to set up the session. He was nice but not very personable. He let me know right away that this is a simple task, and this is the curable cancer. This is always 100% positive results. I trusted him and his promises: *Don't worry she will be fine.*

"Will this hurt her at all? How will she be during and after?" I inquired. He told me she may lose her hair and she will be weak but with exercise and diet she will do fine.

"She's young and strong. It should shrink the mass and she can return to her normal life," the doctor stated.

I believed it. I always wonder if I truly believed the way I do now, would I have put her thru the next seven months of agony- and I mean agony.

I immediately braided her hair thinking if I don't comb it, it won't fall out. It fell out by the braid after the first three sessions of chemo. I went with her for every session. It always took 4 hours. I asked why so long, and I was told that one of the medicines in the treatment was very harmful and if it was put in too fast it would burn her skin. She was always nauseous and very tired.

I never left her side. She went once a week every two weeks. My brother came to visit, and she asked him to cut off the rest of her hair neatly, so she didn't look so crazy. It was hard but she made it easy to do whatever we had to do. She didn't want anyone else to cut it, but Uncle Frank She never wore a wig. Just a baseball cap and her jeans and converse sneakers. She was a tomboy for real.
Her little sister Jenail [Fatty], whom we now call 'Lil T,

was two at the time. She had a great influence on her, and she made her feel good about her hair cut. She told her she looked pretty, and that's all Tanya needed.

Throughout this whole ordeal, Lil T kept Tanya's spirits up.

Tanya also dealt with constipation during the sessions. She would go so long without moving her bowels that twice I had to take her to the hospital because of impaction.

My poor baby had to endure the doctors removing the feces manually, and I mean manually. The first time was awful, but the second time Lil T had to convince her to go.

I got so frustrated when she didn't let me know she hadn't gone to the bathroom consistently. One day she called me upstairs to help her move. The thing is she asked me to pray with her. I ran a tub of warm water and I prayed for her, and she moved. She had the biggest bowel movement I'd ever seen. It was so hard and so big I had to place it in a bag and dispose of it outside. But she sat in the tub and said thank you for holding my hand and praying for me. Well, that was a first. After that, she always prayed with me to help her pull thru this torture. She was bringing me closer to God without even trying.

I watched helplessly as she lost weight and strength. She was a bit of superfluous all her life, but this was real. I still believed she was going to get better. She always made a big deal out of a cold or a fall. So, I didn't take this the way I should've.

When I would take her to her treatments and she came out staggering and being Tanya, I would allow her to fall into the back seat and throw up. I never let anyone clean her. I always picked up after her.

One time she was laying in the back seat and Tupac's "Dear Mama" poured through the speakers. She lifted her head up just enough to tell me that she wanted me to know that's how she felt about me. Of course, I know all the words. To this day I say my Tanya dedicated that to me.

The very last session was in June 1995, and we went for the last time. She had learned to depend on God and was praying for everyone. My sister came to visit, and she and her husband got into an argument and proceeded to leave. Tanya called them back. Of course, they came back because it took all of her strength to get up. She held their hands and prayed outside of the house and they cried together because her prayer was so beautiful. So much love and sincerity was heard, and she believed what she was saying.

Finally, we went to visit the doctor, the oncologist for the end results. It was all good news. He said the chemo worked. He said she was finished and with exercise and good food she would be back to normal in no time. I said, "Are you serious? So happy to hear this news!" -forgetting God's warning whispered to me shortly after Tanya's diagnosis.

So going forth I started bugging her about getting up and moving around. "You have to exercise to get better," I would attempt to encourage her to follow the doctor's orders. She never got up, she just lay there and kept throwing up. I got so frustrated, I'm ashamed to say now. I thought she was just milking it, so to speak.

We finally got the bill from the doctor that did the biopsy. I opened the letter with reluctance, only to find the bill was zero! Yes, a zero balance. I couldn't believe it. I went to the office to talk to the nurse about this and I asked if it could have been a mistake.

She assured me the bill was accurate, and just shrugged her shoulders and said, "That's what he said."

I took it to Tanya and said, "Look what God has done now. Wow. This is unbelievable!" But this was only the beginning of my miracles and ultimate awakening.

I watched her as she tried to be happy, but she was so tired. She looked like she gave up hope. She'd lost 80 pounds and she was getting weaker and weaker.

We had to see the oncologist the next week and he assured me she was just being lazy. He actually said that. I believed him and got angry with her. Wow.

I was angry with her because he told me she should be getting better, and she is not because she was not trying.

July 6, 1995. She was laying on the sofa constipated. My first reaction was, to question her decision to wait so long to tell me once again. In my frustration, I stormed out the door and said to my daughter, without compassion, "If you don't get up off that sofa, you are going to lay right there and die."

Famous last words...

My husband pulled me out and told me I needed a break. So, we went to a motel for the night.

I laid there relaxing and not thinking of anything important. Then there was a knock on the door. I said, "Who knows we are here." I looked out the peep hole and there stood my sister-in-law with tears on her face. I thought something happened to my brother-in-law. I opened the door and she immediately asked for my husband. I thought everything but the right thing. If you ever received bad news, this was the worst.

I kept asking what's wrong and she kept saying let me talk to Eddie. I said is it Cliff [her husband and my husband's brother] she just kept crying.

Through my insistence she was finally able to utter Tanya's name. I stopped -just like I did just now while writing. I will never forget the next moments.

I walked away to the end of the balcony and stood by the wall in total disbelief. "No no no!" was all I could muster the strength to speak. She followed me out and told me she was sorry. I asked, "What, did she go to the hospital, what happened!

Again, she said, "I am sorry."
Again, the phrase "No, no, no!" came sprouting out of my mouth.

All of a sudden, the realization hit. I stood and looked up. I saw three shining arrows coming from the sky. They were headed straight for my heart and when they hit, I instantly felt the pain. A single shot to your heart without breaking the skin. I understand that feeling too well. Immediately, I folded in half and my husband grabbed me. He held me so tight, but nothing could stop nor explain the pain.

Still in disbelief, I remembered the last words I said to her as I left the house in frustration. All because I believed the doctor and not God who clearly told me He was taking her home. But God swam in and out of my life with vivid light and I still doubted his ability to communicate with me personally.

I never thought I was worth the voice. He showed himself from that day forward.

We went to my house and the police were questioning my mother because Tanya's passing was suspicious. I couldn't see her; however, I knew she was still on the sofa. They would not let me in my own house.

They had to question everyone that was at home. I wasn't one of them because I had to get away. I am so sorry for that and I still wish I would have hugged her and said I love you. If I haven't learned anything I learned to remember to say I love you and never end your parting with anger.

The next day I called my job to see what could be done. No insurance- no money for burial. My husband immediately got busy trying to raise the money. But my job had another plan. I informed them of the passing of my daughter and what can I do. The voice on the other end said, "Let me see. Let me call Dallas." She put me on hold and another friendly voice asked if she was in the house when she passed. Now mind you, I hadn't worked there for a year yet they helped me. The voice plainly said, "Put her on the policy." I was sent a check for ten thousand dollars. Second gift from God. My husband didn't believe it and neither did I. No insurance policy had to do this after the person passed.

Then it was time to make the arrangements. The hardest thing to do is talk about how to bury your child. I was numb. There was no place I could go for comfort. I didn't want to see anyone but my kids.

I went shopping for her clothes and a dress for me. Funny while you're in it you don't know you are walking on a cloud.

I went into the store with no money in my bank account yet, but I needed to get something to wear. I found the perfect dress and it was marked down seventy percent. I thought this is awesome and then my thoughts were, *hey this is for my daughter's funeral.* My heart sunk for a bit but crying was a luxury I couldn't afford at this time. I went to the jeans department. and found the perfect outfit. Jeans, a t-shirt and a baseball cap. I was questioned about her attire but, that's all she wore. Why would I put a dress on her now? She never wore dresses. People don't know what to say. I've learned how not to speak when it comes to losing a loved one. I read the book of Job over and over and it seems when he was going thru it, it was best taken when his friends sat in silence with him. It wasn't until opinions seeped in when they started to argue. I've learned how to hold a mother's hand and just hug her, for there is nothing you can say to her at this time. Nothing. Anyway, I wrote a check which I knew would bounce but I would take care of it later. God took care of the check. I never heard from the store and the check never hit my account.

Gift number three and proof that The Most High was driving the car and I was just a passenger. All I had to do was trust.

I felt compelled to continue working at the bank out of pure loyalty. What they did for me was unbelievable. I worked my way up to business cards and handling my own accounts. After five years the bank announced they were opening a branch in Dallas.
I was shocked. I said in the meeting, "We already have a branch in Dallas." But I was assured we didn't. I thought back to the day I called my job to tell

them my daughter passed, and I was told to hold while they called the office in Dallas. As I said before, the voice on the other end said to send me a check after connecting to the Dallas office and speaking with someone. But there was no branch in Dallas! I knew then God had his hand in the pot and I didn't trust him. I trusted the Doctors and the promises of them curing my baby. The promises that the chemotherapy would help cure her. The doctor's advice that she was lazy and I needed to make her exercise. Make her walk and move around. This led me to treat her as if my fussing could make her better. My baby was transitioning, and I didn't hug her or kiss her or simply make her feel better.

My last words to my child were and I quote, "If you don't get up you are going to lay right there and die" – end quote.

The only promise I assumed I had in the bag was that she would outlive me. I thought that was expected. But the real promise was, I'm taking my child home and you will be taken care of.

Never underestimate your worth. You are God's child and He will shake trees and blessings will fall if you reach out your arms and listen. You will walk in this world knowing who you belong to and your only job is to obey and trust because God truly speaks to your heart.

Truly.

Anna

Joy inside My Tears

Have you ever been so broken that you don't even recognize the pieces of your own heart? With tears in your eyes and a smile on your face you try to piece them together like a jigsaw puzzle. Each piece leaving a splinter in your fingers as the memory of what once was or what could never be is played in your thoughts.

I realize I have to free myself from myself. I have to let go of all the should've, would've and could've in my life. I must forgive the only person that matters. Me. I must move on and take care of what truly is— the shattered pieces of me. I carefully pick up the good parts and glue them together with my tears. As impossible as this sounds, I am fully committed and aware that it must be done.

See, God, you told me that I am fearfully and wonderfully made, and because you knew me before the foundation of the Earth, I am going to speak life into my brokenness even as I am getting myself back together. This time is going to be different for me! I understand that my words have power. I am not waiting until I feel better to be better. I am believing and praising the Lord right here in the middle of the pain as these tears roll down my cheeks that I am already better! Even though it doesn't feel good, I guarantee God is going to fix this. It is not bigger than Him nor is it bigger than me. Lord I need to learn as you always remind me that I am yours! You challenge me daily to trust you. All is not lost. It is when I am weak that I am strong. Those moments allow for you to get in the room and fight for me. You are my rock and shield. God sees my tears and fill me with hope, love, and joy. I've found peace, acceptance, and rest inside of your promises. Now I can finally just be... Me.

This feeling of emptiness causes me to feel as if I have nothing to leave this world. The memories of me will fade once those who knew me die. Being a mother allows you to leave a little piece of you that will continue for generations. My nose, my smile , my love for plantains will fade away like footsteps in the sand. So, I cry.

When I was younger I would say I don't want any children. I was the youngest of 3 and got stuck babysitting all the time. No idea my words would hold such weight.

At the age of twenty-four, I was told it would be difficult- if not impossible for me to conceive naturally. See, I was told that my reproductive organs were filled with fibroids of all sizes. I cried because I didn't understand why this happened.

Be fruitful and multiply. It sounds easy until your body betrays you in secret. The one thing I should be able to do as a woman I can't. The one thing I never thought I wanted I couldn't have. So, I cry. Year after year your family asks "When you going to settle down and start a family?" They remind you of your age and say it's only going to get harder the longer you wait.

Not knowing the pain each word they speak inflicts. Not knowing the tests, the scans and procedures I've tried to fulfill this simple command. So, I cry.

Then one day while doing my yearly exam. Waiting to hear the new depths of my bodies betrayal I learn that all fibroids once seen are no more. Could it be that my body finally aligns with the desires of my heart?

I pray and wait for the day that my tears will bear fruit. They water the ground and give life to the seeds I've planted. I can't wait for the day when I can hold my blessing. My promise. Knowing that I wasn't forgotten. That I wasn't betrayed but delayed for God's perfect timing.

Now I cry, I shout and I pray. This delay did not come to stay but to teach me. God is in control and I must have faith in him. I have to stand on his word. Not what I see, not what I hear, not what I feel- just what I know. He did it for Sara, He did it for Hannah, He did it for Elizabeth and He'll do it for me. Now I shed tears of joy knowing I'm next.

-Anna

Tekeisha

Proverbs 18:24
"A man that hath friends must shew himself friendly: another is a friend that sticketh closer than a brother. -KJV)

Toxic Friendships

Have you ever heard the saying, "if it is always YOU, or someone doing something to YOU, YOU are the common denominator?

In toxic friendships, it often occurs that when individuals have a problem with almost everyone they come in contact with, they may battle with their own personal "internal problems" (i.e. low self- esteem and attention seeking.)

"To my people who struggle to voice their opinion regarding friendships, it is not what you say- it is how you say it, don't feel guilty for expressing your feelings."

When thinking of friends we think of happiness, trust, fun, someone that you have grown up with all your life and have deep history, the person that you can trust even when you are not around? Is this person someone that picks you up when you are down, the person you can feel the energy when something is not right, the person that never tells you that you are wrong, the person that is only an ear when drama is going? As it hurts to think and write about, friendships have promises that are often broken; and it leaves a bad taste in your mouth when it comes to trusting others. You build the bonds and stick close, some of us have friends from childhood; but let us not get it twisted, history has nothing to do with loyalty! Read that again! You could have known an individual for fifteen years and another person for two years, if you ever had to question your friendship at all with your long history friends, and or just someone you defined as a friend, then quite naturally it was not friendship from the start. When you are a genuine person, your character will never go unnoticed, others will observe your actions and behaviors that you present. We all know that if it is in your heart, it will come out. It cannot be hidden. I was that person for many years, always seeing good in others, but I was only hurting myself. Dealing with resentment and trust issues in the past, I hope I can help you open your eyes to notice signs early.

I remember talking to my Aunt about a friendship that was unstable and toxic, yes let us not be oblivious and think that friendships cannot be unstable and toxic. My Aunt explained to me she also had gone through a similar situation in her previous years. I discussed with her that I thought this person was a friend, I had genuinely thought a lot of the person and loved them just like they were my own biological sister. Shoot I can honestly say I treated them like a sister. I noticed some of the signs earlier in the friendship but refused to go with my instinct, giving the person the benefit of the doubt. What I didn't realize was that not being aware of patterns and overlooking them; would only cause a continuance of unhealthy behaviors. I can remember coming up with excuses for friends when they showed unhealthy friendship signs. For instance, never taking accountability for anything, If something happened between us like a miscommunication, a fall out occurred. It was almost always NEVER their fault. I would think to myself, like seriously, some of this stuff you have to be responsible for, take ownership for your wrongdoing. Fess up and own your stuff! Be mindful and watch for the patterns, never go along with something that does not make you feel good about yourself, speak on it! I told Auntie, some of that with others had been going on since high school years, yes high school and continued as an adult. In high school is where we all know cliques are formed, we all know that!

I recall a time where I ended up being disliked by some of my true friends, peers, and other people in the area, due to others wanting to choose sides. We all know that there are three sides to a story, yours, mine and the truth! Some people had to fall on the side with who they felt was giving the best story, the side that where they knew the other would/wouldn't be upset with them, sugarcoating and playing victim and the list goes on. Some "friends" will believe they never did anything to cause anything.) Yeah okay, their audience did not even believe it, but to keep the peace with the person they sided with the speech that was given to them. I know you may say, "Well goodness, that was high school!" I will say to you some things never change, only time.

Some of these actions continued, sad but true. I explained to Auntie that some of the pain that I felt in the high school years, and even some of my early adult years was really gruesome. I would often wonder why people really would go along with what one person stated. Like, this is really toxic! I can recall being disliked by so many people in my own little town and how others would say, "you know better," "what did you do?" I know what you're thinking..., "draining" right??

It took a lot of praying, talking to trusted people about the situation and growth to realize that nothing about this friendship was good. Do not get it twisted, it did not happen overnight and I still often felt deceived. (Don't give up here, keep seeking to find out what is healthy! Find and set boundaries!) I heard some of the apologies that were given with no actions to back up what was said. I fell for promises stating the behavior would not be repeated, I didn't mean it that way, and so forth. I know this is hard to talk about, for some of you, but I know you can relate. I took that and often believed that things would change. It sounded good. I believe that a toxic trait that I have is always allowing people to come back regardless of what they have done. I have grown and no longer choose to be around anyone who made me feel like I was the reason behind every fall out, situation, or circumstance. Do not get me wrong, I am not accusing the "friend" for everything, there were times that if I felt the energy or vibe was off, I backed away especially at adult ages, I do not have time for that! I give people their space when I feel something is off, that goes for EVERYBODY! Protect that peace Sis/Bro do not feel guilty if you need to remove yourself from others.

People as you read this and think of friends that this may pertain to, remember that it is okay to set boundaries early and walk away in love and no hard feelings. You may hear all sorts of things about what you did and you are such a bad person, but your best coping skill will be keep a positive attitude, attempt to discuss the issue (this takes two people to engage in a conversation and everyone is not ready to have "those" conversations), try not to accuse, be true to yourself, do not get caught up in the "messengers." Remember, if they know that much, why did the friend feel so comfortable talking around them? Those are just some pointers. Yes, it will hurt, because you felt as if this was a "friend." Be mindful of utilizing the word "friend," it is okay to have associates. Watch for the signs and remember that you do not have to go through this.

Competition, y'all how many of you can relate to this? I know that's silly right, to think about this word with friends. Well let us not forget that if a person is toxic, competition may surface. This can be seen in friends, family, or foe. I can only speak for myself, I have never competed with friends or family! I usually compete with myself to become better! We all have the same amount of time in a day- go get it! I have the mindset that if you are my friend, if I have it you got it and everything I do for you is from the heart. Sad to say, you should be aware and mindful of the patterns that may present themselves as competition.

Take your power back people, if you are experiencing things like this from "friends" "associates" etc. choose to be happy and not engage in anyone or anything that will heighten your anxiety and cause you to react out of character! I sat back in silence and observed, always remember that every action doesn't require a reaction. One of my favorite quotes, "You are destroying your own peace confronting everything you peep." Just let 'em have it." I saw it, I heard it, I did not confront it. Do not think this is a sign of weakness, it is a true sign of GROWTH! I refuse and I won't do it, and there is still no love lost I promise. I just chose to love from afar. You can too, do not be afraid and do not feel guilty.

Auntie shared with me the time she was awarded with something, and her friends didn't show up. It reminded me how I continued to make others a part of some things that were celebratory to me and they chose not to attend, which is okay now that I realize that the people who were there were the people who are supposed to be there. Do not get upset!

Everyone won't and cannot celebrate with you! I didn't understand that until a couple of years ago. I am so content at my adult age and time of my life that I do not and will not put up with such nonsense anymore from anyone who displays those actions and poses as a "friend!" You can do it too. As I began to observe the behaviors continue year after year, friends this year, falling out the next two years, I had to get a backbone! I honestly know that those behaviors are DRAINING! I know and you know all about those behaviors. I removed myself and continued to sit back and watch. And yeah, you know I say, well maybe I should have gone out of the way to have a conversation with them, but like I explained to Auntie, I was exhausted just by thinking to myself what the hell is it now? I don't know what happened, was it miscommunication? After a while you've got put that mess to the side and realize that there are people who project their feelings on others. I felt that I made the best decisions to walk away in happiness and not anger. Now I am not saying go and search the heart of every friend that you have and try to point out this and that flaw. We all have flaws, but you will feel genuine true friendship, you won't have to force it. Like the old saying goes, how long you have known a person does not define the loyalty of a person. Genuine people cannot hide that they are genuine, it just happens. Friends make a promise to be there regardless of the situation, you communicate, give space, be honest and get through it! Don't feel bad for checking in with your feelings. If it don't feel right, it isn't right. Always remember that you are unable to change people regardless of who they are. They must be willing to change themselves.

Friend(s)

They say true friends are always there no matter what, times get hard we work that out...

You will always connect to the people that are

genuine from the start, never overlook the flags, I promise if you do, you will have a broken heart.

Broken heart because you put too much trust in a person from time and time again, just to realize that you really are not true friends.

Yes, arguments and bickering may occur, speak on the situation not twisting the story to fit your needs. Do not bring others into the space, it causes them to act funny and really they should just take heed.

Friends do not make an effort to have others look at you like you are an awful person, because of a falling out, they address the issue and make amends and that's no doubt.

Attempt to be a true friend with no hidden agendas in mind, love me like a sister or brother because true friends are hard to find.

Written with love and peace. Keesh

Tracy

My Truth

Everyone has *Broken a Promise* or two or three in their lifetime. But for me, my broken promise changed my life, my firstborn's life as well as my change of life baby. I made a promise to my child to be the best mom I could, and I fell short on my promise. Let me go back a little. My name is Tracy, and I am a recovering addict. I have struggled for many years with heroin and crack/cocaine addiction. ADDICTION means being addicted to a particular substance, thing, or activity. There are many people addicted to things such as sex, alcohol, shopping, gaming, partying...the list goes on. They are all treatable, the person just has to be willing to change. Change is hard for a lot of people. Substance abuse is a treatable, chronic medical disease that can become deadly for some.

I can't blame my addiction on anyone except me. I was trying to be a part of a world I knew nothing about. Peer pressure is real, and this is where a lot of people get caught up using drugs. I am an only child from my mother and the oldest child from my father. I was raised by both parents, for the most part in a loving and caring home. My grandparents played a major role in my life because my mother and father were very young when I was born. Growing up, I'd never been hungry, homeless, or went without. I could say I had it better than a lot of others. I went away just about every summer and had a beautiful childhood. Because of my addiction, I have experienced hunger and homelessness. This was something new to me and I did not like it. Shame and guilt kept me using for a very long time. I finally gave myself a chance after being arrested several times and went into treatment where I started working on myself and issues that I felt were holding me back from moving forward. It was no one's fault I became an addict and I had no one to blame for my own shortcomings.

While in treatment I met the man of my dreams. He was handsome, tall, well-mannered and had good sense of humor. He loved me and my shortcomings. See, when you become addicted you lose yourself sometimes, and my self-esteem was at an all-time low. So, for someone to look at me and like or even love me felt so good because I had stopped loving myself. This man was also in treatment, which was strictly prohibited, because one of the first things they share with you is no relationships especially during the first year. Rule number two was no dating another client while in treatment, but again this was the man of my dreams so of course I didn't listen. This man was my King and by any means necessary I was going to make this work. I was not willing to walk away. Well, I ended up getting kicked out of treatment for something else, but we continued to see each other while he graduated from the program. We got an apartment together shortly after him completing the program, and a few years later we got married.

After getting married, I got pregnant. Neither one of us had children, so we were so excited about bringing a new life into this world, our world. At four months pregnant I had an appointment to find out the sex of the baby. We both couldn't sleep the night before because we were so excited. Well, things didn't go well at the appointment they informed us that there was no heartbeat, and we were heartbroken. We were both broken into pieces, barely speaking to each other because we didn't know what to say. I personally felt less than a woman because I fell in love with this man, and I really wanted to start a family with him. I thought because I had some female issues in the past that I would not be able to have his child. I also thought I was being punished by GOD because I had been pregnant before in another relationship and I got an abortion. My thought patterns were all over the place. We both fell into a state of depression and as I stated we were distant with each other. We NEVER spoke about that day again, and just decided to move on.

A few months later, on the same morning I found out I was pregnant with my first born, he was accidentally killed by a gun - a victim of gun violence. Well, they say GOD has a sense of humor, but I didn't find any of this funny at all. I felt like I was having a bad dream waiting for someone to wake me up. I didn't know what direction to go because I felt like I didn't get clean and married to raise a child by myself. I didn't want to raise my child without a father, making their life complicated. I know women do it all the time, but this was not what I wanted for my child. I was five years clean at this time. I didn't tell anyone about my pregnancy, because I was unsure of what to do and I didn't want anyone to talk me out of not having this child. I finally told my family I had decided to get an abortion and my aunt was so upset with me. I had an appointment for the next day. My aunt told me to go home get on my knees and talk to GOD, that He would lead me in the right direction. And that's what I did. I went home got on my knees asking GOD to send me a sign or help me make the right decision. I set my alarm clock and it didn't go off at 7 a.m. I woke up around 11 a.m. and that was enough of a sign for me. I decided to have this baby and love it enough for me and him.

I had a beautiful baby girl- but to be honest I was scared to death. I had no idea what to do with this new life. I didn't want to ask for help but I got lots of help especially from my mom and her wife. This baby did not sleep so I was always so tired because I would stay up with her. After dropping her a few times, I learned to get some sleep. It was very rewarding being a mother, but that didn't take the fear of being a mother away. I need to say because I found out I was pregnant the same day my husband died I never really mourned him. I was always told what you feel your child feels and I didn't want my child to be sad.

I'm here to tell you if you don't deal with your issues, they have a way of dealing with you. I went five years without mourning this man and when I decided to go to grief and loss therapy, I couldn't handle it. Shortly after my second session I ended up using again. Using trying to hide it from family and friends and raising my daughter at the same time. That didn't work out for me. I have to thank my mother and her wife again for taking my child, giving her a loving home, and doing everything I wasn't able to do because I was using again. The guilt and shame kept me out there using for another four or five years (I lost count.) I was so lost and felt worthless because I put a substance before my own flesh and blood. The disease of addiction is real, and I was caught in its grips. It had gotten so bad that I was taking my child with me to buy drugs and taking her places where I used, sitting her in another room with some toys. GOD was truly looking out for both of us because a lot of things could have gone wrong.

After my mother had my daughter, I tried a few times to get clean but was not successful, so I decided to move to another state. That didn't work because I wasn't ready to surrender. I continued to use, got married to another addict, and it was off to the races again. After about a year of marriage I got pregnant, and then got locked up. Here I go again, back in jail now I'm pregnant trying to figure out what to do. Well things worked out for me. I was sentenced to a program for mothers and their children. I was pregnant, getting the right care and learning how to love me again. By the time I had this child I had made a promise to myself, my first born, my unborn child and GOD that I was going to get it right this time. That was almost fourteen years ago. Things haven't been easy, but I have not used and have been able to be a mother to both of my children. I feel like I cheated on my daughter. I sometimes feel she feels the same way because my second child has never seen that side of me. So, I want to publicly apologize to my firstborn

KENNEDY letting her know I am your mother no matter what and I NEVER stopped loving you. I am so sorry that I couldn't keep my promise to you. I know I missed out on a lot of things, but you need to know I will always have your back, I love you, I adore you and I admire you for the woman you have grown up to be.

I want to apologize to my son because of my past. He and his sister have grown up in different households making their relationship difficult to a certain degree. My son didn't know much about my past, not that I'm ashamed, but he has so many other things to deal with I didn't feel the need to tell him. I know my children love me, but I still feel like I am being judged sometimes. Not necessarily by them, but just for being a free spirit. My life is an open book. If I did it, I'll let you know I won't lie or turn a blind eye to the things of my past. I keep positive people in my life and everyone in my life must have a purpose. I love GOD, myself, my children, family and friends but during this journey called LIFE I have had to disconnect with all negative forces that were in my presence. One of my favorite sayings is "some people are in your life for a reason, a season or a lifetime." I allow people to pick their position depending on how they handle me. Because of my life experiences I don't allow anyone to get in my way, not even those two beautiful children I have, and I have taught them the same. Learn from my mistakes and anything you desire in life, if it's positive go for it.

-Tracy

Katrina

A Promise Broken...

Since the beginning of my existence life has been very different for me. I truly believe I am to be the creation made to live a life that included some serious trials and obstacles. I was to live through them and survive only to be able to tell others my story serving as an inspiration which will help them to make it through whatever they are facing. Although my story may not be your story, and I may have questioned time and time again, why me, it is still a testament of survival regardless of the challenges we all experience in life. My life from the beginning has seemed to have many broken moments and broken promises. I could be here all day telling you story after story about how I was let down or how some things just didn't work out the way I expected or planned, but I won't bore you with all of that. I think the best thing to do first is to tell you a bit about who I am.

So, who am I? Well, I was born and raised in a single-family home. Just like most of the other stories we've heard in the past. One of the first broken moments I experienced was being raised by my mother with only seeing the man that produced me a few times in my life. This was so difficult as a little girl seeing other people with their fathers, but never having yours show up to protect you in any situations you may have faced. I know this may sound strange, but I've accepted the fact that although I wanted and desired that full daddy- daughter relationship that's just not how my life played out. My father had his own demons to face so he didn't have the capacity to be there for me the way he may have wanted to. There's a time in life you may have to face reality and say, "my father's job in my life may have been to just get me here." He fully served his purpose, and I'm not mad nor do I hold resentment towards him. If it wasn't for him completing his assignment, I wouldn't be here writing this today. I know we've all heard the old famous statement that says, "people come into your life for a season to teach you different lessons." I believe that to be true even when it comes to the parents that created you. I believe a parent's job is to get you to the end of their assignment and then that's it regardless of what that assignment might be. It could be just to meet your mother, create you and leave forever. It could have been your mother who met your father who had a one-night stand that made you. Your mother may have given you a way to another family to love you and give you what you need in life to survive. That of course may seem harsh and unfair, but if we were all born with the perfect life scenarios then what would set us apart or make us any different than the person sitting next to you?

Another broken moment that took me by surprise and almost broke me permanently was the loss of what I thought would have been my love forever.
Let's start at the beginning of how this all occurred...

You have found <u>the</u> one, lol... or at least so you believe! You've convinced yourself that you've come across that person that is going to be there till the end through the storms of life and hold on to you no matter what may come. The one you thought would fight with you to push through this relationship journey. The one that would stay in the ring with you to fight just as hard as you, because you're both determined to make this work. That is when not just the thought of rock bottom hits, but when it actually does.

How we connected so quickly is truly unexplainable. Let's just say it was an overwhelming romance. I was basically swept off my feet by the thought, the hope, and possibility of endless love. The first conversation we ever had lasted from the wee hours of the morning till night with very few breaks in between. I truly had the feeling that this could not be more perfect, and it could be the moment that I finally found my person for life. Conversations were about life, love, God, children, business, dreams-just everything you could think of. We connected in such a way that has never happened to me before. There was an instantaneous connection that was unimaginable, a pure magnetism. We began dating within one week of getting to know each other, and yes, I know what you may be thinking that you can't love someone that quickly. However, I disagree. Love for me doesn't have a timeframe or a time requirement. Love is a **_choice,_** and we chose to love each other almost immediately.

As our courtship progressed, I was involved in every aspect of his life from knowing all his personal information from day two to helping him with his investments within four days of meeting each other. He must have really trusted me to give me all of his personal information. I knew his social security number and bank account information in such a short period of time. He told me he's never found someone he could trust so quickly, and never thought this was possible. He had given up on the potential of love due to his past relationships and how they had ended. In all honesty I really wasn't looking for anything, but I had done the work prior to his arrival as if he was already here. It wasn't long after that I began to see myself within his family structure and given the opportunity to meet his children. Coming from being an only child to having a full family meant the world to me. I've always wanted and loved having children around so the addition of his seven didn't bother me in the least bit. Being an only child and coming up all alone put my heart in the position to want and desire a large family. So, meeting the six out of seven of his children was a wonderful experience, feeling like I could finally create the family I've desired. I met the kids and their mothers within three weeks. I was added to school records and able to pick the kids up whenever I wanted. I was able to build a good relationship with the mothers where they could trust me with their kids. This was going so well you couldn't tell me this wasn't the plan of Christ, because it was all working out just like I had hoped it would for years. It was going so well that I became friends with the kids' mothers. We called and checked up on each other outside of my ex- husband being around. Those types of relationships don't normally happen often at all. You usually hear about drama and contention within those types of relationships, but that wasn't my story.

We kept moving along as a blended family and enjoying the newfound love we had all come across. He and I talked about the homes we wanted, the businesses we were going to start, the vacations we wanted to take alone, and the ones we wanted to take as a family. I received poetry almost every other day and he spoke some of the sweetest words I've ever heard. We developed cute pet names and could stare into each other's eyes and just know what the other was thinking. He made me feel like I meant the world to him, and this was going to be life forever. All of a sudden, three months into this undeniable love, he asked me to marry him. My heart stopped and I couldn't believe that he wanted to marry me and make me his wife. I told him we could wait a year and not have to rush it, but he was starting a new life on the road, and he didn't want to leave this up to chance and lose what we had. So six months after our proposal was our wedding day. Now don't get me wrong it wasn't all bliss when it came to him and I dealing with each other, but the things I didn't like weren't major so I could live with it. Now my family on the other hand didn't like the idea of us. Everyone had their reasons why they felt this was not the one, but I was going to make my own decisions and live with whatever came along with it. I was put under so much stress and given so many reasons by everyone why I should reconsider marrying him. At one point the stress became so bad I was hospitalized with pains in my heart. The doctor had told me that if I did not stop stressing it would kill me. We were both faced with some serious setbacks very early in our dating phase, but we were both there for each other.

This sealed the deal even more that this was the person I wanted to spend the rest of eternity with. No matter what he had my back. It was just difficult finding the love of my life but being told not to do it by family and realizing you were going to have to walk this road alone without any hope for support from those you love. I remember going into my room and praying and asking God to confirm three things for me and if He would confirm, then I would marry him. I never spoke any of those words out loud, but by the time I walked down the stairs he had answered every one of my questions. The only reason I needed this was just because of all that was being told to me, and from everyone's thoughts about him. So, after counsel from a spiritual covering and the confirmation I received, I said yes.

As I prepared for my celebration, everything I could think of from the venue, my dress, to the cake, the food, and seating was done by some of my closest friends that I considered my family. My sister's friends or "my lifers" as I loved to call them; although they may have had their own reservations, pushed to make sure my day was special and I had everything that I needed. The wedding was beautiful and full of laughter and tears. We had done it. We beat the obstacles and got married. We were looked forward to beginning of an amazing journey. We went back to our suite laid in each other's arms and took a sigh of relief. Before we fell asleep, we talked about what we were going to accomplish next. The next step for us was for him to go away to start the trucking business. I was willing to give up everything to help my love achieve his ultimate dream. It didn't matter to me what I had to sacrifice. All I wanted was to ensure my love accomplished everything he put his mind to, and it would also secure our future. I could eventually do the same and as a cohesive unit, we could accomplish all of our dreams. We didn't know that it was going to happen so soon. We got married on a Saturday and on Sunday morning we woke up to a message that said his truck was ready and he could pick it up and start working. We were both elated, he asked if it would be okay and of course I said yes to ensure that he started his dream, but that of course would be okay because this was for our family, so I was all on board. He left on Sunday night to fly out to go begin our life. That is where I truly believe was the beginning of our end. We never had the opportunity to fortify a bond between us as a married couple, and this allowed a lot of things to get in our way. Although we had professed our love for each other and promised we would be in this for life, I truly found out that promises are just words, and they can truly be broken.

This wedded bliss and love filled courtship kept going for a bit even with him being on the road full time. Although setbacks kept happening, we knew this is where we wanted to be and the two of us would live happily ever after. Of course, we were aware that nothing is perfect, and trials and tribulations would come to invoke the core presence of our love, but we didn't care. We knew wholeheartedly that we had someone that would go toe to toe with me to make this love last. Well, that is until a raging financial storm hit our doorstep like a tornado, and hurricane all mixed together. This seemed to put the biggest strain on our relationship, and I was left in the rain and wind to figure out how to get through. I had to maneuver without any help of the ultimate love that had weathered the storm with me in the past. We then started talking less. When we did speak, it was with contention or distress. A financial storm in a relationship can truly show you who you are and what you're willing to put up with. Although your vows say for richer or poorer, no one really considers the "for poorer" part of the vows as an actual option. This truly defined who we were.

It's those trials that make us and mold us into who we are and the existence we create. I personally don't believe anything is done by accident or by mistake, everything is done by divine intention. If we begin to really realize this, then we may stop blaming the parents that we feel didn't do their job. We may be able to move on in life and complete the assignment, we were given. In every aspect of our lives if we realize the ones, we blame may have really completed the job they were intended to and moved on to the next assignment of their life. Instead of us realizing that we hold on to resentment, disappointment, anxiety, and frustration because life didn't work out, the way we thought it should. WHO EVER SAID IT WAS SUPPOSED TO WORK OUT THE WAY YOU THOUGHT? Surely God wouldn't let me go through pain, stress or heartache. We must remember that although we have freedom of choice, we're ultimately not in control of our lives so all things happen for a reason. God may have allowed this to happen to teach you something that you can share with someone else. A prime example is the one I went through to write this to encourage you to look at your situation in a different way. You may be facing this test to be a testimony to someone else. It's funny we all say "Lord make me a testimony", or "Yes God, I want to see miracles", but if you don't have a problem for him to fix what do you need the miracle for? You must go through something in order for you to have a testimony. We also say "Use me Lord," I said it and He used me to endure this situation in order to have a testimony to share with you. It took me a lot of time, but I recognize that things I know or feel I may need may not be what's best for my life and may not assist in the progression of my existence. Okay enough letting me try to counsel you...

Now test your faith point... When thinking of the situation I expressed, what would you do?

WOULD YOU:

(A)   : Hold on to someone that potentially doesn't want to hold on to you, but you believe in God and the vows you committed to. Besides, you know love can come in phases and you have a large capacity to forgive and let go. You also remember the words that were spoken about the blessing of your union and how it would be a help to others.

(B)   : Set fire to his work vehicle because deep down you feel: *how dare you let me help get you where the heck you are, and now when I really need you you've disappeared. You decide to bail out and forget your priorities*! (I think I might have a deep- rooted violent side...Lord help me! Lol...)

(C)   : Let it go and walk away going back to the independent, self-reliant, making it all about you person you could be. Forgetting the "us" and thinking only about the you.

(D)   : Allow a few of your brothers and sisters to do a sneak attack while you take every dime that they have so you can feel vindicated.

Your first choice is a great indication of where you are in life. I originally chose C, but God had another lesson to teach me even in this situation. See, I was great at telling you the story of how my husband broke his promise to me, but I didn't really talk about how I broke my promise to him. When promises are broken a lot of times regarding relationships there's always two sides and you don't really look at how you pushed the person or gave the person the ammunition they needed to move on with life. Although all of those things I stated did happen in my relationship, God had to shine the light on me and remind me that in every argument I explicitly said to him if you don't like what I said then *divorce me*. If you don't like what I'm doing then *divorce me*, if you can't stand my actions *divorce me*. So, when I got that phone call, and he said those words that he didn't want to be married anymore why was I surprised? Why did I become angry, blame him, and wondering how could he do this to me? See- it wasn't only him breaking his promises to love, honor, and respect my marriage. I broke my promise by continuously telling him he had the right to leave me. So, he did!

I remember being in a very dark place after our relationship ended and having to start all over. I cried all the time and kept wondering why he would do this to us. YOU PROMISED ME! YOU KNEW I NEVER WANTED A DIVORCE! After I had my time of self-pity, and I was finally able to see things clearly that's when I was faced with my reality that I was a part of the brokenness and reason that this happened. I went through this lesson to truly learn that what I say matters, and I can truly have whatever I say. I realized the moment I spoke those words I broke the promise I made to love, honor, and respect all the days of my life.

A lot of times it's hard to look at yourself and the actions you've caused to have this situation go the way it's going. See what we forget is we truly have the power of life and death in our mouths. Let's consider the law of harvest. The principle is you reap what you sow. So, if I'm saying the words, "divorce me" then I reap a divorce then I shouldn't be surprised. If I sow the words, "there are no good men or women left in this world" then I reap never finding a good one. I shouldn't be in shock. If I sow the words, "I'm always broke" then you reap never having any money whose fault is that? See in all these scenarios **YOU ARE** the problem by just what you're speaking not anything or anyone else. It's your confession and your true heart beliefs. So, you shouldn't be surprised when things aren't or don't work out how you'd like them until you first examine what you put into it. Take a true look at what you're confessing out of your mouth. See if you truly are the promise breaker or was it just someone else…I bet if you stop and look in the mirror you'd be surprised by your reality.

-Katrina

Sheila

Full Circle

I was at marriage counseling when the counselor said to me, "people usually marry someone just like the parent they struggled the most with". I think that that is accurate. At least for me it is. Growing up with a mother who was a narcissist, I grew accustomed to the pain of not feeling loved, especially in the way that I needed to feel loved. It doesn't make sense, rationally, that you would be drawn to that type of love. But as I look over at my life, and all of the decisions that I made, I can see where it all comes from. My very beginnings. I could see where I never felt love from a young age from the person that I needed it from the most.

I can remember being afraid of my mom. I did not receive actual love from her, but I was also afraid not to love her. She would be angry if she ever found out. I would pay. We would all pay. So, I got used to the feelings. Those feelings felt like home. Without a shadow of a doubt, I always yearned to have a mom like some of my friends. I gravitated towards friends' houses where I felt that love that a family should feel. My mom would always tell me that we had a great life compared to how she had it growing up. She was the real victim. And I promised myself from a very young age, that I would be different. That I would love my children, and there would never be a time when they thought I did not love them. I wanted all of it. The husband, the house, lots of children, and even a dog. That was my fantasy. I wanted to have a family that I loved. The thing about growing up in a house where there was physical and verbal abuse, is that you live life afraid. You are told at a very young age, what a bad person you are. What a bad child you are. I think I was around 10 years old and like many 10-year- olds I had a group of friends and one day they stopped talking to me. I have no idea why. I could not figure out what it was. I came home and my mom asked me what was wrong. I told her all of my friends were mad at me. She asked why, inquiring about what I did to cause them to act that way. I indicated that I had not a clue as to what the issue was and they refused to talk to me, her response was accusatory. "Well, you must've done something or else they would not have been mad at you," she replied. Her response made me feel worse than I ever felt. I wanted comfort and reassurance, yet all she had to provide was accusations and chastising.

I remember when people would come up to my mother and compliment her on what well behaved children she had. She would respond "That's because I will beat their ass if they don't behave themselves!" I was constantly ashamed, and consistently felt that I was not worthy of her affection. When I was eighteen, I worked a full-time job during the summertime. One summer Saturday morning I was sleeping in a little bit because I had been out the night before with friends and my mom came in my room and told me to wake up because that was the day, I was supposed to be wiping down the walls of the house. You see, she smoked, and the walls of the house had that yellow dingy look of nicotine. The house always smelled like an ashtray.

I was always ashamed that I too smelled like cigarette smoke. My mom would get angry at me if I asked her not to smoke in my room. She would look at me with hateful eyes and tell me that she was not a dirty animal, and that she would smoke in her house wherever she wanted to. But that day in particular, she told me to get up and start wiping the walls down. I confirmed her request, but fell back asleep. A short time later she came back to my room and started hitting me. She smacked me right out of bed. That day I decided that I would move out of the house, and I would never come back again, even if it meant that I would live on the street. I always had a pretty good relationship with my father, but one thing about my dad-he always stuck up for her. I guess looking back, it wasn't so much that he loved her that much or believed in how she treated us, but he had to live with her. He had to stick up for her, and he never stuck up for us. I don't know how I feel about that today. But I know that it damaged my self-worth. So very shortly after the day when my mom beat me out of bed, I gathered all my things put them in my car and went to live with my older sister.

All of us kids had our struggles because of my mother. We all have our own stories to tell and ways that we coped with our childhood. But I always knew that I was not her. I promised myself that I would never be her and I would be the mom to my own children that I needed. That was a promise that I would never break. Time went on and there were probably a couple of occasions where I was about ten bucks away from living in my car. But I always made it work.

I always worked hard and tried so hard to never look back. I forgave my mom a thousand times, and a thousand times she did not disappoint by continuing to be hurtful and abusive. As I grew older, I got stronger. I got to make my own decisions, but never stopped trying to have a healthy relationship with my mom. Even fifty-three years later, I still try. She never disappoints in testing my forgiveness.

I still continue to forgive, because I honestly don't think she knows how to have a healthy relationship with anyone. I can only look at myself in the mirror and tell myself "You are not her," and that advice was reinforced by a beautiful friend of mine who struggled with her own relationship with her mother.

Hindsight truly is twenty-twenty vision…the treatment I received from my mother would be the blueprint of the treatment I received in relationships for years to come. I was twenty-three when I met him. That was the year that my best friend got engaged. One thing about me, I couldn't wait to find my happily ever after. Growing up like I did, caused me to have big dreams. I had dreams of becoming someone's wife. Dreams of becoming a mom. When I started dating Joseph, I would go to his house on the weekends because he lived about an hour away. I would clean his house, take his laundry to the laundromat, and cook for him. I'd do all the things to show him what an amazing wife I could be. I just knew that he would love me and everything that I had to offer him. Every day I would prove to him how worthy I was for him to love. About a year later we decided to move in together. I gave him all of the wife privileges with the promise of forever. We had our fights, because I felt like I did all of the "women's work" with little to no help from him. I felt like the maid. But he had a great job, and he was going places. I kept telling myself that he could offer me everything that I never had. I didn't know then like I know now, love was one of those things that I needed and never had. My vision of love had been distorted.

After a year of living together, I gave him an ultimatum. I can tell you right now that rule number one should always be that you should never have to give an ultimatum for someone to want you or to love you. Back then all of my friends were getting married and having babies. That was the life that I wanted more than anything. The way that Joseph loved me was the way that I was used to being loved. It was me trying to show him how amazing I was and that I was worthy of his love. Cooking and cleaning? Wasn't that part of being a good wife? Isn't that taking care of your man? These are the things that I would tell myself never realizing that it is not love. But, the ultimatum for him to either put a ring on my finger and marry me or that I would leave was one that I made. In my heart of hearts I really wanted to believe that he didn't want to lose me. He knew I loved him and would do anything to make him happy. So, one night he got drunk and got down on one knee. He asked me to marry him and I said yes. Later I would make jokes about the way he proposed, about him being drunk, but inside it hurt. I accepted it because of my self-worth. In my mind that was what I was worthy of. I had my ring. Now it was time for wedding planning-the fun part.

I knew that my parents weren't going to be able to help financially and from the beginning his parents said that they would. So I got a second job to start putting away for my share of the wedding. He came from a very big family and the wedding was very costly. His parents had the financial means. We had to cut back on some things. For example, he told me that since I didn't have a lot of money, I could not spend a lot on a wedding dress. One day I went to a wedding dress event where they put everything that wasn't purchased on sale. There were so many dresses there. I had to go by myself. I had a very small budget, and I knew I had to stick with it, or he would be mad. I picked out a dress. It didn't look like any of the dresses that I had dogeared on my *Brides* magazine. He told me I couldn't spend a lot, so I spent a couple hundred dollars on a dress that I really didn't like, but it was the one that I was worthy of. He told me it would be OK because it was only for one day. The days of planning the wedding, and the decisions that I always dreamed about making for my special day? Well, because I didn't have a lot of money, Joseph, let me know that the input would come from him and his family. He went to register for the wedding with me. My friends wanted to make a day out of it. We would have lunch and go pick out the things for our first house. But Joseph told me that he didn't trust that I could pick out things that he would like, so I had to go with him instead. He chose the China pattern. He did not like the dishes for daily use that I picked, so we had to compromise, as he put it. Everything was a compromise- mostly on my part. He reminded me that his family was paying most of the wedding, and that he was buying a house, so that gave him a reason to take make the decisions. He told me how lucky I was to be having this big wedding and be able to move into a four-bedroom house. And I, knew deep inside that it didn't feel right. None of it felt right. But I was on my way to have my very own family. I could not wait for the day when I could love my very own baby and give all the love I wished I received. I was afraid to marry him and I was afraid not to. In the end the longing to love and be loved brought me to the altar for my wedding day. I questioned myself as I stood across from Joseph with the priest to the left side of me asking me to repeat after him. He wanted me to make the vow to love Joseph, and honor him all the days of my life. In my head, I repeatedly asked myself *what am I doing*? To the right of me were over a hundred family and friends who came there to watch me say I do. So that's what I did. I said I do. The next day we left for our honeymoon and two weeks later I found out I was pregnant. This was not on Joseph's timeline. He did not want to be pregnant right away. I did not think it would happen so fast. We were getting older, and a few of my friends were struggling with fertility. We had made a decision to not use any protection. We figured that if it happens it happened. We were married, and it would be alright. Years later, he would say to me, that he never agreed to that. Even though he knew that I was not on any kind of birth control, years later he would blame me for giving him children that were not on his timeline. When my son was about a year old, we went away to celebrate our first anniversary. Joseph had just gotten a new job which required him to travel Monday through Friday. So he would leave Sunday night and come back on Friday nights. The job had a salary more than twice what he was already making. So we were going to celebrate our anniversary, and his success. We went away to a little cabin in Virginia. When we got home, something told me that I might be pregnant again. Sure enough, we bought the test on the way home, and I took it right away. Indeed, it was positive. He was not very happy about it. Much like the first time. We made the decision, early on when I became pregnant, I would quit my job and stay at home with the children. I had been working full-time, and my oldest was going to daycare. With Joseph being away all week, whenever the baby was sick, I had to stay home, and we were paying more for daycare than I was even making. It made sense for me to become a stay-at- home mother. That was a decision that later he would throw in my face and say he never agreed. He would claim he was not a part of the conversation. That conversation never happened. I would always refer to my journals. I have been writing my thoughts down in a journal since I was sixteen years old. I wrote everything down. Even though I would show him that I wrote down conversations that we had, he would accuse me of writing down things that I thought happened, but never really did.

I think it was later in my pregnancy with my second child that Joseph started cheating. I didn't know it then. I always suspected it; I would write in my journal all about his behavior. Him constantly picking fights so he could leave for a few hours. He would come home from his work trip and pick apart everything I did and didn't do. All of the signs were there. But he would tell me that he was not cheating, and that I was crazy. His job was certainly convenient. He had his freedom, and he was able to do whatever he wanted and be in a hotel room with whoever he wanted. He would leave on Sunday night and I got to be a mom. The one thing that I've always wanted to be in this world. We would have a phone call every day. And on Friday I would make sure that the house was clean and dinner was on the table. I would make sure that the kids were taken care of so that he wouldn't be mad at me. I would start to have so much anxiety on Thursdays because he came home on Fridays. He would go over my receipts, making me account for every penny spent. I would have to explain expenses every week, as he was my auditor. Then there would be the fighting, and me walking on eggshells until Sunday night finally came. I remember one morning begging him to at least let me get out of bed before he started telling me why he was angry or how I was messing up. I became pregnant with our third child and his anger and disappointment were palpable. I was happy, and yet I was exhausted being a mom. If I asked him for help with the children, he would tell me that I would have to figure it out because this was the life that I wanted. He would get so mad at me and I would try even harder to not make him mad. We finally went to marriage counseling. Later after my divorce, I would find out that at that time he had been in a relationship with someone who he worked with several states away. He told me that he told the marriage counselor separately. But he never did tell me. I know that there were quite a few more in all of the years that he traveled. I never really had a chance. I could never compare to the other women who had nothing better to do than to just give him everything he wanted in the bedroom. Certainly not raising his babies and taking care of his home. They thought he was amazing. And I'm sure they thought I was a frumpy lazy wife, who always had a baby on her hip. Even to this day, I wonder what he told them about me. Our marriage counselor was amazing. And I honestly think that he was able to get through to Joseph. For a while things got a lot better. I felt like he finally appreciated me. Everything that I did. I started to feel safe talking to him, especially when the marriage counselor was present. We tried to have a go at it without the counseling. It was very bumpy, and after I found out that I was pregnant for a fourth time it became even bumpier. I was definitely surprised, this one I had not expected at all. I was so afraid to tell him. I was so afraid of what he would do. Over the years our arguments became so volatile. He knew the things that would scare me and he would utilize all of the tactics. There was more than one occasion where he was physically abusive. He cried and promised it would never happen again.

Our marriage was in shambles, and I never knew how I was going to come back from that. Later he would stay true to his promise but just stop short of hitting me deciding instead to corner and block me from being able to leave the situation until he was done spewing hateful and shaming words. Now here I am pregnant again. When I told him, he asked me to call the doctor to see what could be done about the pregnancy. I did as I was told. My doctor got me in right away and before we did any testing, I went into her office. She asked me what was going on because she knew this was something that I would never do. I told her that my husband was very angry with me and did not want me to have another child. She asked me what I wanted to do. She knew the answer. All I could do is sit there and cry. I was terrified. Once again, my marriage was in disrepair. here I sit with a baby growing inside of me that my husband wanted me to abort. So she told me that she would not do it. Partly because she knew it's not what I wanted. They brought me into the sonogram room to see how far along I was. When they did an internal ultrasound, they found the sac but they did not find the baby. She told me that I was probably going to have a miscarriage and that I should come back in another week so they could look at measurements and see. She said at the time the sac was measuring about eight weeks pregnant. I knew that I was pregnant, I knew that I was not going to miscarry this baby, and I told her that I knew there was a baby in there. We made an appointment for the following week and I went home and I called Joseph. I told him what just happened and he said he was relieved. I hated him at that moment. I told him that we were going to check again, and that by nine weeks we should be able to hear a heartbeat. I went back the following week. We did another internal sonogram. Again, there was no baby, but there was a sac and it had grown. She ordered some blood tests to check my levels. Again, I went home and called Joseph and I told him it was the same news. My doctor had mentioned getting a d and c but I refused. I knew that I was pregnant. The next day they called and told me that my hCG levels were indicating a pregnancy and that I should come back in another week for another ultrasound. Joseph encouraged me to have the D&C. I told him I would not. But he was so sure that I was miscarrying that he didn't press me on the issue. The following week I went back again, and we had the same conversation. The sac was growing, and they still could not find the baby. My doctor said there was only a ten percent chance and that we would give it one more week and then we would have to have a serious conversation. So, I prayed, and I ask God to please help me. To please give me this baby that I so desperately wanted and already loved more than anything. I remember driving to that appointment the following week feeling like I was going to a funeral. I went into the room and the sonographer had a little bit of a sad face when she saw me. She said, "When I saw your name as my first appointment today, I prayed for you." It was the day after Thanksgiving. I got ready and instead of an internal ultrasound, she put the wand on my belly and she made a funny sound and she took the wand off of my belly, with tears in her eyes, she looked at me. She put the screen towards my face and put the wand back on my belly. She said, "Here's your baby, and here is the heartbeat." I cried so hard. I was so thankful. I was so blessed. I got my pictures and I went home. Joseph was upstairs in bed with one of the boys watching TV. I sat down next to him and he could tell I had been crying, so he thought that there was no baby. I handed him the pictures, and He asked me, "What is this?"

I said "that's the baby."

He said "you're actually pregnant?"

I told him I was. He spent the next nine months resenting me. He was never going to make things easy on me, but especially now. Though I was very much alone in this pregnancy, I was excited to find out I was finally having the daughter that I had always wanted. God blessed me with a daughter. He never wanted to feel her kick. He never wanted to go to any of the appointments or sonograms. I had three very active boys, I was homeroom mom, I taught catechism at the church, and I was very much alone in my marriage. To this day, so many years later, I struggle to forgive him for that time in my life. I wish that it could've been different, and I could've had those hallmark moments. I wanted all the firsts with a man who was in love with me. After my daughter was born, she was playing in the playroom, one day, and he came into the kitchen, and he apologized for never wanting her to be born. She loved him and, a part of me thinks that it hurt him how much she loved him. It was at that point that we went back into counseling. We were clearly just going through the motions, and we both had so much resentment towards each other. I wanted to make my marriage work. I wanted to have that family that I never had. I would've done anything to save our family. So back to counseling we went. We went through some hard times where Joseph lost his job. Financially, we would be okay for a bit, but it was very stressful. I was prepared to work at a convenience store, whatever I needed to do. He got a job that would allow him to not travel anymore. The caveat was that we would have to move a couple of states away. It would mean that I had to leave everything and everyone that I loved. My family and my friends. Everyone. But I thought I could save our marriage if we were in the same state. Although he never admitted at that time that he had other women in his life, I knew that I would be able to control that equation, so I chose to move and leave a home that I loved, leave my family and friends and move so that I could work on my marriage.

There is a line one of my very favorite movies "we are the decisions that we make". I think of that over and over again. I think that in the moment we make the best decisions that we know to make. The trajectory of our lives are really based on that one moment. But I had the best intentions in saving my marriage and saving my family. Having a family was the most important thing, above everything else that I ever wanted. So, I found myself very far away from home and everything that I knew and loved. For the first time since I was a child, I felt lonely and without anyone. I felt like I had no friends and that no one wanted to even know me. It was a perfect opportunity for Joseph. Looking back it's easy to see the narcissism. The act of taking someone away from everything that they know in order to control them- this is what I was experiencing. Many times, I wished I could go back in time and change that girl who was uncertain and scared and lonely and tell her *you can do this*. I threw myself into the kids more than ever. My oldest son had a difficult time adjusting to middle school. But we threw ourselves into sports and doing our best to fit in. Joseph had already lived here a year while we were trying to sell the house back in Delaware, so he was very much acclimated. He was very much into relationships that more than likely were inappropriate. After all, he was the same person in Delaware as he was here. I thought that I was being the best mother and wife that I could be. But the control and the fights continued and seemed to get worse. I was not allowed to handle anything with the new house. I wanted to move into this house and pick out some furniture and paint the walls and make it our own instead of me feeling like I was living in some other lady's house, that I did not even like. I didn't even get to choose the house that we bought. He found a reason to disqualify the houses I liked. But I wanted to make the most of it and make it ours. Joseph tightened the reins of control. He picked out the furniture, and I got to look at what he picked before he ordered it. Decorations, pictures, knickknacks... that was his job too. He would not allow me to paint, because he liked the colors of the walls so he deemed that not necessary. Within a couple months, we had a very big fight and I realized just how much control over my life that I had relinquished to Joseph. The fight was pretty simple. I wanted to be able to text friends and family on my phone. Texting cost five dollars a month and Joseph let me know that since I did not work outside the home I did not make any money. Therefore, I could not afford the five dollars a month for texting on my phone. Of course, he had texting on his phone because he needed it for work. Also, then he allowed my oldest son to have texting on his phone as well. I told him I was done and finally he acquiesced. That was probably one of the first times where I realized how deep I had gotten in this abyss. As time passed, I started making some friends with other moms on baseball teams. It was obvious that Joseph was not very well liked by the other parents of our children's teammates and friends. As I looked back, I realized all of our friends that we've ever had, were our friends because of me, and that the friendship with Joseph was by default. It wasn't till after my divorce that I realized how much people thought that he was just a pompous ass. It broke my heart to hear how people would talk about it, and the control and the way that he treated me. My friends were delicate about it. A friend one day commented to me that she had seen Joseph in the store and said, "Hey, all of the girls are getting together. Can you see if Sheila can come out and meet us on Thursday?"

His response was, "Well, we will have to see, I guess as long as she has dinner ready before she goes it should be fine."

She said to me that initially she thought he was joking and then quickly realized that he was not. He became the topic at the dinner table that night, and that planted the seed. I came to the conclusion that I loved my family, but I did not like him at all. I started noticing more and more the things that he would do to manipulate my thinking. I started noticing what marriage should look and feel like. There was a time when he was having a lot of sexual dysfunction. I was really worried, thinking that he might have an illness, cancer or something serious happening. I implored him to see his doctor and discuss it. It took months and months for him to finally go, and in that time our sex life was almost nonexistent. When we did have sex, it was over within two minutes. Finally, he listened to me and went to the doctor. He came home and basically blamed me for his condition. He told me that the doctor told him that I would have to give him oral sex daily to get his libido up, and that I would have to be more open to things like anal sex in order for him to be satisfied enough to maintain an erection. I was devastated. With the struggles that I had with my self-worth this added so much. He told me that it was because of me. Eventually he admitted that he was only joking, but for days he blamed me and of course, I thought it was my fault. The doctor did give him the little blue pill, and it took him over six months to fill the prescription because it cost too much. It felt like our sex life was not worth the money. That I was not worth it. Today I find that very funny, because what it actually cost was my feelings for him sexually. So I found myself sleeping in another bedroom, drifting further and further from the control and constant battle for my self- worth. I threw myself into the kids, and every day I became more numb. I did what I could in my marriage to keep the peace and keep him as happy as I could. I think the catalyst was the day that my brother took his life. That was my lowest and darkest day. Joseph had no idea how to be there for me. The more he refused to love me and support me through my grief, the more I began to despise him. My brother taking his life was a lesson for me. He taught me that you only get one life and it is up to us to decide how are we going to live it. I made up my mind with such resolve.

With my youngest starting school, it was time for me to get a full-time job so that I may provide for myself the best way that I could. That began the fire in me to get out of this dangerous liaison, my marriage. I wanted to be a better example for my daughter. I wanted to show her that I could be strong. It took all of my strength, and I had to borrow so much strength from my friends to persevere. It was around the holidays following my brother's death that I told Joseph that, I had had enough. I wanted a divorce. We decided to stay together until after Christmas so that we could give the kids a good Christmas. He asked if we could go to counseling and actually made me believe that our divorce would be friendly, and that he only wanted what was best for me and for the kids. As the hundreds and hundreds of times before, I believed him because I wanted to believe him. He convinced me that we didn't need lawyers that we could just go through a mediator to finalize terms of our divorce. Weeks were going by, but he was not doing anything to begin the process with the mediator. By this time I had not shared a bed with him in about two years. He was drinking, and he was smoking, and I was not. I also had not been attracted to him for more than two years. I think, when a woman divorces a narcissist, they come to a realization that the person is a monster. I think that day when I realized that he was having me followed in order to catch me having an affair was that day for me. In the state of Virginia, if you have divorce proceedings brought against you because of adultery, you could make the case that your spouse does not deserve any spousal support. Now, this was a slap in the face for many reasons, notwithstanding that he spent our entire marriage cheating on me while he worked in other states. Always making me feel like I was crazy when I knew and questioned him when the signs were apparent. So instead of the amicable divorce, he served me with papers on the grounds that I was the cheater. He misconstrued anything that he could in order to make it look like I was the cheater, just so that he could make good on a threat that he issued me years before. He told me that if I ever left him, I would be living in a cardboard box on the street without my children. I fought for over two years spending well over fifty thousand dollars on lawyers. I was fighting for my life, and if it wasn't for my best friends, especially Pam I would've never made it. I would never have had the strength to continue to fight. During the time that we were going through the court system continually made it very difficult for me financially. He would make decisions to not give me any support at all, he did not care if I was able to feed the children or not so that he could prove that I could not take care of them, and he could make his case. But my friends would not let me fail. They came through and lent me money and made sure that I had everything that I needed. Thousands of dollars. My friends told me to keep fighting and not to let him destroy me. Finally, the day came where the judge saw fit to give me alimony for life-the one thing that Joseph fought the hardest for and tried to ruin my name in order to make sure I got nothing. The Judge gave me my life back. Although he granted Joseph the divorce he saw Joseph's tricks a mile away. I fell to my knees and thanked God. God saw me through it. He surrounded me with people who would not let me stop fighting for myself and most of all for my children. All of the prayers were answered on that day in May. Now it was time to put together every single promise that I made to myself and to my children. Three months later, I sat at a table and started signing papers. Those papers were to buy MY very first house. I found the best house in the best neighborhood that my money could buy and I provided for my children something beautiful, a new beginning.

That very first weekend, we celebrated my children's birthdays. A group of friends came over and helped me paint. I got to paint my house! I got to choose my furniture. I got to make decisions for myself and nobody could take that away from me. It's going on four years in my house and there are so many days that I sit there and look at how far I have come. I admire the peace that's in my home, and I am so grateful to God for putting an army around me that supports me to this day. I still continue to take a high road with Joseph. It's the best thing that I can do for my children. But they see who he is. And they see who I am and I know that I have made them proud. I still work on trusting men and I know that one day my time will come and I will meet the man that I will spend the rest of my life with. For now, being the mom that I want to be... the woman that I want to be and living in a home that I made a home surrounded by so much peace and love was worth it. There are times when I hear him echoing in the back of my mind, "you know nothing"... "You have nothing"... "you will never be anything without me"... but I can look at myself, and how beautiful my life is and know without a shadow of a doubt he was wrong. So wrong. I have thought about these words. They are still so raw to write. This is my truth. It may not be the way he recalls it, but it is my story.

-Sheila

"...their hearts are steadfast, trusting in the Lord. Their hearts are secure. They will have no fear; in the end they will look in triumph on their foes"
-Psalm 112:6-8

Meet the Authors

Katrina A. Payne

Katrina A. Payne, known lovingly to her family and friends as Trina, KAT, or KP. An only child from New York, she is a vibrant, fun-loving, giving, tender soul who you can always find smiling and laughing out loud even in the toughest situations. Katrina is known for always seeing the silver lining in everything and everyone. She is the proud mother of one son whom she adores and loves spending time with. Katrina is a dynamic individual with a passion for knowledge and communication. She was born with an insatiable curiosity and has always been drawn to the world of ideas and possibilities. This life educated woman has a genuine enthusiasm for learning, she's continually seeking to expand her understanding of the world and its intricacies. In addition to her love for knowledge and creativity, Katrina possesses exceptional communication skills. In her professional career within Social Services, she has honed her ability to articulate thoughts effectively, whether through engaging in public speaking, writing compelling narratives, or fostering meaningful discussions. Her empathetic nature allows her to connect with individuals from all walks of life, embracing diverse perspectives and valuing the power of dialogue as a catalyst for positive change.

As the owner and CEO of K. Payne Management she believes in helping small businesses and is deeply passionate about helping others by assisting them with driving continuous improvement. Katrina possesses a growth mindset, constantly seeking opportunities to learn, evolve, and stay abreast of industry best practices. Her dedication to staying ahead of the curve empowers her to introduce cutting-edge tools, technologies, and methodologies that optimize processes and drive organizational success. Katrina's love for writing started at a young age as an escape from the world around her. That escape has produced several writings about life, love, and trials which she is putting together as an encouragement to woman about how their past mistakes is not the determination for their future.

As Katrina continues to embark on her personal and professional journey, she aspires to leverage her knowledge, creativity, and communication skills to inspire others, foster meaningful connections, and contribute to the betterment of society. With an unwavering dedication to lifelong learning and a genuine desire to make a positive impact, "Katrina is poised to leave an indelible mark on the world."

Anna McLarthy

Anna McLarthy is a career driven woman with over 15 years of healthcare experience. She is a member of Zeta Phi Beta Sorority Inc and enjoys being a "Finer Woman." Anna migrated to the United States with her family at the age of three. Though she has no children of her own she is surrounded by a host of nieces and nephews that love her unconditionally and view her as a second mother. Anna always enjoyed writing in her diary but never thought she would ever publish her thoughts for the world to see. Being a co-author of Broken Promises brings her great joy, because she knows that her pain mirrors an experience that will help others overcome their own. Every day in her walk with God she learns just how much He loves her. God's word never fails she says. You are what He says you are. Don't let the enemy tell you anything different. When times get rough Anna encourages herself and others through God's word in **Psalm 139:14** "I am fearfully *and wonderfully* made."

Sheila Colon Cacciatore

Sheila Colon Cacciatore has always had a passion for the written word. Her thoughts spill onto the page honestly and from the heart. She has been journaling since she was a teenager – writing down situations, emotions, and reactions. The catharsis that came with it was not lost on her even at a young age. Fast forward some 35 years later - words have just as much meaning. As a now confident, genuinely happy, and divorced mom of four, she spends each day striving to live her best life. She hopes the words she shares with readers help them see that everyone has their own battle and that they are not alone.

Kiara Samuels

Mrs. Kiara Samuels is a Licensed Mental Health Profession, a Licensed Chemical Dependency Professional, and Licensed Master Social Worker. Additionally, Kiara obtained a certification as a Mental Health First Aid (MHFA) trainer. While this is her first experience as a co-author, it is just the beginning of Kiara's journey as a writer. Kiara is big on faith, family, and love, and has found joy in being able to help others navigate through life, rather good or bad. She has a passion for empowering youth and has a proven track record as an exemplary role model. In addition to providing therapy services, Kiara started a group for young women called Inspire to be Inspired where young women can come together and express themselves while working through life challenges.

Lauren Staples

Lauren Staples is a healthcare worker, writer, and single mother who was born in Detroit, Michigan, in 1980. She spent most of her childhood in Wilmington, Delaware, where she developed a passion for helping others.

After completing her education, Lauren began working in the healthcare industry, where she has spent over 23 years helping patients in various capacities. Her dedication and hard work have earned her the respect and admiration of her colleagues and patients alike.

Despite the challenges of being a single mother, Lauren has never let that stop her from pursuing her dreams. She has always been passionate about writing and has recently begun writing about her past relationships and her faith. Drawing from her own experiences, she hopes to inspire and encourage others who may be going through similar struggles.

Lauren's life has been a testament to her resilience and strength. Through her hard work and determination, she has overcome many obstacles and continues to make a positive impact in the lives of those around her. She is a true inspiration and a role model for anyone who wants to achieve their dreams, no matter the odds.

Tracy Bolden

Tracy Bolden, born and raised in Jersey City, New Jersey has worked for over 20 years helping people who struggle with alcohol, drug addictions as well as mental illness. She is passionate about helping others because she knows what it feels like to be in need. It's important for her to give back what was so freely given to her. With this being her first project, Tracy is excited to share this piece of her life; negative and positive, for the person or persons who are waiting to hear her testimony that will be the motivation that will encourage and set them free as God has done for her! Tracy loves spending time with her family, friends, and community. Tracy is a God-fearing deaconess in her church, and she also helps the less fortunate in her community.

When reading her story, she shared sacred parts of her life that she is not proud of; however, lessons have been learned. She would not be the person she is today without some of the shortcomings that she has overcome, and there is still much work to be done. Her desire is for every woman who reads her story understands how important her broken promise is, and how much more valuable she became once God restored her life.

Jeanetta Loveberry

Jeanetta Loveberry is from St. Louis Missouri raised in Delaware and recently relocated to Ohio in 2017. She is a mother of beautiful three kids. Through the years Jeanetta has faced challenges from being a teenage mother in high school, going through a divorce, and being a single mother all while trying to figure out life as an adult. Writing became her escape to getting through hard times, expressing her true feelings, and motivating herself to achieve her goals.

On her personal journey in life to live in total peace and happiness, Jeanetta found it very uplifting to inspire all walks of life. Some of her unique ways made an impact on others' lives by sharing her own life experiences on how she overcame those obstacles, making people laugh, and even a simple word of encouragement from her heart.

Jeanetta is a busy person outside of being a full-time mother to her 3 beautiful kids. She owns a cleaning business, is a Travel Planner (travel agent), and of course, she is an author. Jeanetta is by far a phenomenal woman who is determined to help and inspire others to live their best life no matter what obstacles they may be facing in life.

Tureka Dixon

Tureka Dixon was born in Boston, MA. She is a tradeswoman, an avid outdoors lover, and a mother of two who loves spending her time with her sons. She has worked in the building trades for 18 years. She started as a laborer and later joined the Glaziers Union to obtain her degree in construction management. She is a certified Union Glazier and currently serves as the recruitment coordinator for her local union. Tureka spends time outdoors, taking hikes, bike riding and just listening to nature. Tureka has a creative side; she has the ability to create unique gifts for family and friends. She also enjoys cooking for her loved ones. When Tureka is not at work or attending her children's sports events she loves to meditate, she believes that peace and quiet are essential for your well-being.

Tiffany Alston

Tiffany Alston is a woman conquering life through Christ! She is a mother and now grandmother who finds great joy in those roles. Originally from New Jersey, she now resides in Delaware working daily as a Clinical Policy Analyst and nurse. She has a passion for breaking women free from anything attempting to rob them of God's plan and purpose for their lives. Tiffany is always open and honest with other women so they can see that even in their uncertainty they will still see God's presence. Tiffany has successfully managed teenage motherhood in her life, becoming a widow in her early twenties, and now a divorcee. She has endured emotionally through many different stages in her life but refuses to allow anxiety and depression to defeat her. She believes in the total wellness of the spirit, body, and soul. Tiffany has led in advocacy for special needs children and nursing needs at the state level. She has led the Graced Women's ministry, is a current team member of the Seeds of Greatness healthcare ministry and continues to meet a need wherever she can. She desires to love people past the things holding them back, so they can see that God's love is greater than any past pain!

Chantel Bratcher Coleman

Chantel Bratcher Coleman resides in Newark, Delaware with her husband, five of her children, and eleven Cane Corso's. She is an educator, licensed therapist, and the CEO of a private practice for mental health.

Her love for literature started at a very young age and has continued into her adult years leading her to have a passion for education. She is an advocate for mental wellness and social change in the community. She has been recognized for her contributions in the field as a Women in Business honoree, Family-Owned Business nominee, and NAACP Legacy Award winner. The author has been compelled to tell her story to show that everyone can benefit from the process of healing. No matter how many traumas and setbacks you have lived through, sharing your story is the beginning of a release and reset. She believes that we all have the potential to reach Greatness once we are able to accept our truth, overcome obstacles and start living in our purpose.

Janie Mitchell

Janie Mitchell was born in Philadelphia to uneducated and spontaneous parents. They often played by the rules only if it were their rules. Her parents raised their children like weeds, and with Janie being the second child of seven, she quickly became the overseer of her siblings. Janie's mother played by ear, and as a result, was very dysfunctional. Her father had a good job but didn't know how to lead his family without force. When Janie's parents separated, Janie became the babysitter after school was out. She got pregnant at the age of 15 by a man named Larry. During this time, women who got pregnant didn't go to school, they got married. Her mother signed for her, and his mother signed for him, the families brought the new couple a house fully furnished, and the two were left without further instruction on how to care for their newborn child. Janie's newlywed husband Larry became abusive soon after they began to stay together. She imagined her new husband got his parenting skills from his father while she got her submissive talents from her mother. Larry began working to support their family at a mushroom factory and would come home every day bathed in the smell of the fungi he worked with. While Larry was off at work, Janie cared for their child. At the age of seventeen, she was pregnant yet again and very familiar with the abuse Larry put her through. She lived in constant fear of underperforming or leaving tasks unfinished because her husband would abuse her if things were not to his liking when he returned home from work. This was the story of her life. Always trying to please others while putting herself last. Now sixty-nine years old, Janie is finally finding how to search for herself in a maze of fear and uncertainty. Her hope is to reach someone while they are young enough to take advantage of the power within, the possibility of removing the taught mask and reaching the innate talent hidden by doubt and ignorance. Janie loves herself now but wishes she knew herself better years ago. The light inside of her is finally on and her God- given strength is emerging. She is finally unafraid to speak up and say she is important, she matters, and she is relentless.

Monique Taylor Gibbs

Monique Taylor-Gibbs is an educator in born and raised in Wilmington, Delaware. As an educator for over twenty years, she is embarking on her fifth year as a school administrator. She prides herself of leveraging the impact of positive relationships to impact student success.

Monique earned a Bachelor's degree in education from the University of Delaware, as well as a Master's degree in School Leadership from Wilmington University. She is a highly decorated member of the community. Her dedication to the success of students surpasses the confines of the school, and she often advocates for the needs of students in the community. Ms. Taylor-Gibbs has formulated her teaching practice and platform while working with students in the city of Wilmington since she was a youth. Identified as a leader early on, she prides herself on being the trusting adult every student needs. She is known for her truth in the delivery of content, high levels of engagement and efficacy, and loving students beyond their own barriers and obstacles. She seeks to incorporate real-life relevance into every lesson and makes sure the students leave her classroom empowered with the appropriate tools for future success.

Writing provides her a sense of release and freedom from the daily hustle. She enjoys spending time with her family. She is the mother to Nycere and the grandmother to Khalan. She wishes to thank her son for being patient and believing in her. Her mother for her support, and Freda, for the huge push. She also thanks others who have helped to cultivate her gifts by reading something she sent in a moment of creativity.

Tekeisha Dennis

Writer, Poet and Author, Tekeisha Dennis born in Salisbury, Maryland on the little Eastern Shore has been putting pen to paper since she was a young little girl. Writing "short stories" leaving them around the house. She has always loved writing short stories and as she became older began writing poetry as a coping skill. It helped with saying the words that she just could not remove from her tongue and helped with the test, trials and storms that she had to face. She is often awakened at night with either words to put on paper or the title of the next poem. Tekeisha has written numerous poems for friends, family and strangers, but has never been published. She has always dreamt of publishing children's poetry books. Tekeisha is an Educator at heart and has a passion for children. Tekeisha is a wife and a mother to two kings. Tekeisha received her bachelor's degree in 2019, and Masters in Social Work in 2021. Tekeisha has mentored children and adolescents and worked in Public Schools and the Mental Health field. Some of her writings are used to help others cope and to find their voice through writings. She hopes that people will read her stories and take away one positive thing.

Michelle N. Butler

Leader, Influencer, Author, and Teacher, Michelle N. Butler from Delaware, was born to a phenomenal woman, the late Sandra Butler Brooks. She entered this world with a charge to lead the youth and women of this broken generation to embrace their potential, uncover their purpose, and give them the tools to become who they are meant to be! Michelle is a woman of great faith and has accomplished many achievements because of the Lord's hand on her life. In collaboration with co-authors, wrote a women's book entitled, *"When Sisters Speak, Life Lessons for Women in Ministry."* She served as the Youth Pastor of New Destiny Fellowship for thirteen years and was recently appointed the Women's Ministry Director. In 2021, she received two honorary Doctoral Degrees from Anointed by God Ministries Alliance and Seminary in New York. Leadership and Administration is a passion for Michelle. She has served as a leader in various capacities and has assisted great leaders in managing their businesses. In 2007, she was selected and honored as a member of Cambridge Who's Who Among Executive and Professional Women. In her personal time, she enjoys hosting Sista-2-Sista Fellowships, which brings women together to minister, empower, and strengthen their spiritual gifts. Desiring to offer the Kingdom of God a "more excellent way" to manage and lead, Michelle received a Master of Management in Public Administration.

Dara Brown Kasabo

Dara Brown Kasabo has a burning love for the medical field. Due to her fiery personality and her passion to care for others, she has made a name for herself as a professional Healthcare worker in Southern. California. She is a Self-employed caregiver in the elderly community.

Dara obtained her Certified Nursing Assistant certificate at San Diego Job Corp Center in 1993-1994. She furthered her education at Pacific Coast College trade school in Physical Therapy and Massage Therapy. Outside of her devoted time to the elderly community, she worked as a preschool teacher for 10 years.

Dara is married to her encouraging and supportive husband, who helped her raise two determined, compassionate, and headstrong individuals. She has also been a mother figure to a host of others as well. Her and her husband have been blessed with two beautiful, sweet and energetic granddaughters.

Dara expresses and explores her right-brained way of thinking. She loves the arts... crafting, singing, dancing, sports and taking anything unfinished, and turning it into a masterpiece. Her creativity has played a predominant role in her life, her career and as a mother and wife.

Freda Camille

Author, Poet, Pediatric Nurse, Publisher, Playwright, Youth and Young Adult Advocate Freda Camille transparently shares her testimony about various adversities and traumas she has experienced in her life through her the many books she has authored.

Fortunately, those trials and tribulations were exactly what she needed to embrace and fully understand her purpose. With all she endured, she gained faith and strength which ignited the passion to be who she needed when she was younger. After releasing her seventh title "Open Wound" in 2020, Freda took a break from writing and began mentoring and coaching aspiring authors about the writing process. She remembered how things were in the beginning for her when God first gave her the vision. Chase the dream was her plight, but she was not sure as to how. Of course, she did her research; however, having someone in the flesh with wisdom and wherewithal to help always makes a difference. Soon she would meet Ms. Em, owner of MeJah Bookstore, Claymont, Delaware, whom was truly God sent! So as Freda gained wisdom, she knew when the time was right, she would give back that which was given to her to aspiring writers and creatives of all ages. She began assisting authors to become self-published through coaching or providing individualized services through her company Chase Zion Publishing. Freda expresses gratitude and joy when she assists authors through the process towards realizing their dreams.

One Woman's pain... is another Woman's experience!

Have you ever been in a situation where you felt all alone?
So boggled in your mind that you cannot pray...
There is nothing to say.
Just cry?
Have you ever needed someone to talk to?
The only thing that you can find to say is "Oh God why?"
Well I am here to share some wisdom;
One woman's pain is another woman's experience.
You are not alone.
God allows tests to come for you to walk through,
To experience the hurt and the pain,
The joy and the triumph...
This causes you to be able to help someone else.
You cannot give advice or
Understand.
Without having gone through similar trials and tribulations.
The tests come in different ways,
But the way to overcome never changes...
God will choose one woman's experience to be the visual aid,
That would nourish another woman's pain,
Help her to sustain and persevere.
Remove the sting and give her revelation,
.... bask in God's glory because morning has come,
Claim the victory.
Now is the time,
You are to hold your head high,
And let the light shine,
Grab hold of God's vision that He has allowed you to see,
One woman's pain is another woman's experience,
It is the essence of the enemy's defeat.

        ©Freda Camille
        2 Timothy 1:4-7

www.ingramcontent.com/pod-product-compliance
Lightning Source LLC
Chambersburg PA
CBHW070647160426
43194CB00009B/1617